SHOW, DON'T TELL

HOW LAWYERS CAN USE VIDEO TO STAND OUT, CREATE MORE VALUE, AND REVOLUTIONIZE THEIR FIRMS

TEMI O. SIYANBADE

AMERICANBARASSOCIATION
Law Practice Division

Cover design by Sara Wadford/ABA Design

Printed in the United States of America.

28 27 26 25 24 5 4 3 2 1

Library of Congress Cataloging-in-Publication Data
Names: Siyanbade, Temi O., author.
Title: Show, don't tell : how lawyers can use video to stand out and revolutionize their firms / Temi O. Siyanbade.
Description: 1st edition. | Chicago : American Bar Asscoiation, 2024. | Includes index. | Summary: "In this book, I will walk through the different components a law firm and how most law firms work to show you step-by-step ways to use video as a catalyst for change and growth. Specifically, we will break this journey into three sections: The Essentials, Video for Communications, Video for Marketing. In Part 1, we will unpack the essentials of incorporating video into your practice. As part of our discussion we will touch on everything from legal ethics related to using video all the way to choosing the right gear and building your unique setup. Then, in Part II, we will explore how to use and optimize video for your virtual conferences so that you experience more engaging and effective video conferences. Finally in Part 3, we will discuss the ways you can leverage video in your marketing and share your videos with the world"– Provided by publisher.
Identifiers: LCCN 2024031722 | ISBN 9781639055241 (paperback) | ISBN 9781639055258 (epub)
Subjects: LCSH: Practice of law–Technological innovations–United States. | Law offices–United States–Automation. | Technology and law–United States | Videoconferencing–Moral and ethical aspects–United States.
Classification: LCC KF320.A9 S59 2024 | DDC 347.73/64–dc23/eng/20240716
LC record available at https://lccn.loc.gov/2024031722

ISBN 978-1-63905-524-1

Discounts are available for books ordered in bulk. Special consideration is given to state bars, CLE programs, and other bar-related organizations. Inquire at Book Publishing, ABA Publishing, American Bar Association, 321 N. Clark Street, Chicago, Illinois 60654-7598.

www.shopABA.org

Contents

PART 3 Video for Marketing

Video Guide Available

As part of your purchase, access to a complementary Video Companion is included. This tool will enable you to implement the action items outlined in this book with ease. Access the guide by visiting www.showdonttellbook.com.

Introduction

You picked up this book because you are interested in video, but there's more to it. You picked up this book because you want to experience a change: a revolution, or at least an evolution. If you're like the hundreds of attorneys I've worked with, you want a transformation in your firm because you want a transformation in your life.

I believe this book about video for legal professionals can be a catalyst for you in that quest. I believe it can be a catalyst for you because I have experienced what is possible in my own firm and life.

HOW VIDEO REVOLUTIONIZED MY FIRM AND LIFE

My journey with video has helped me in ways I could not have imagined when I was a recent law school graduate and baby attorney trying to hang her shingle. I was desperate for clients because the bills were piling up, and my income was sparse. No one knew who I was. I also had no concept of process in my firm. There were moments I felt like I was on an island with this firm and wondered who would rescue me. Somewhere amid that desperation, I found video.

The first time I found myself recording for an online platform was as a favor to someone who is like a sister to me. This sister, a tried-and-true serial entrepreneur, was building a platform where she provided insights about life and relationships to women.

I declined.

I had no desire to be on camera. I was a dignified lawyer, for heaven's sake—not some influencer needing the public's approval. However, after a bit more persuasion, I agreed, and that was my introduction to the world of video. And since then, everything has changed, yet everything has stayed the same.

A part of me still does not want to be *that* influencer. But I have realized that even that mindset is rooted in narrow-minded thinking. When it comes to influence and video, it is easy to create these stories and rules about how we can influence and what it means to show up for ourselves and the people we can impact.

Video creates the opportunity to influence and so much more. With video you can showcase your expertise, increase your exposure to potential clients, and create evergreen proof of the value you bring. As I write this book, I have published more than 70 YouTube videos that have been viewed more than 260,000 times. Sixty percent of my leads have come from these videos. I have also discovered ways to incorporate video into every part of my client experience. From lead generation to referral building, video has helped to establish my credibility, build relationships, and streamline my practice.

Additionally, I have the opportunity to speak on national stages in front of my colleagues, peers, and potential clients on everything from the law to leadership and everything in between. All this has happened, but I'm still myself. I did not have to dance on social media or relive the details of my latest challenge. If I wanted to do those things, I could, but it is not a requirement. Instead, I have helped thousands of individuals find greater clarity in their legal journeys, assisted my clients in understanding my firm's processes, and really enjoyed being an attorney. In short, video has revolutionized my law firm and my life. I believe that it can do the same for you and your practice.

Now you may ask yourself, "But, can this book help *me*?" Maybe you believe that you are too old or not tech savvy. Perhaps you are introverted and feel too shy to step out, or you may wonder how you'll find the time to add video creation to your never-ending list of things to do. But you *can* do it. And by picking up this book, you've already taken the first step.

By implementing the steps in this book, you will find that video can revitalize your practice, establish your thought leadership, and preserve your relevance in the legal industry. You'll find that you have the option to spend more time with your family, opportunities for more disposable income, and repeated systems that help cultivate new clients so that your pipeline stays consistent. Along with that, you will find a path toward a practice that supports your personal goals, too.

These may seem to be audacious goals, but I believe revolutionizing your law firm is possible if one leans on the side of intention and strategically crafts each step.

WHAT LAWYERS DREAD ABOUT VIDEO

Whenever I bring up the topic of videos for attorneys, one of the first emotions I sense is dread. For some, that dread is accompanied by a dash of insecurity. How dare I suggest the pursuit of something as trivial as video when said attorney is on a mission to change the world? In other instances, the dread is accompanied by insecurity: why would anyone watch anything I create? Who am I to make a video on anything, let alone something as weighty as the law? But, taking a line from Marianne Williamson, "Actually, who are you not to be?"[1] Consider your credentials and the people you could serve. You likely have over twenty years of schooling, including seven years of higher education.

Additionally, you are part of a select few. Out of the 333.3 million people in the United States,[2] there are only 1.3 million who are lawyers.[3] In other words, only 0.3 percent of the people in the United States can do and speak about what you have worked toward becoming. You have endured one of the most academically and intellectually challenging fields of study. You overcame that hurdle to sit for an exam that the world recognizes as highly challenging—and you passed. Yet, you wonder, Who are you to speak about your area of expertise?

HOW TO USE THIS BOOK

In this book, I will walk through the different components of a law firm and how most law firms work to show you, step by step, ways to use video as a catalyst for change and growth. Specifically, this journey is broken into three parts:

1. The Essentials
2. Video for Communications
3. Video for Marketing

In Part 1, we will unpack the essentials of incorporating video into your practice. As part of our discussion, we will touch on everything from legal ethics related to using video all the way to choosing the right gear and building your unique setup. Then, in Part 2, we will explore how to use and optimize video for your virtual conferences so that you experience more engaging and effective video conferences. Finally, in Part 3, we will discuss the ways you can leverage video in your marketing and share your videos with the world.

---

[1] Marianne Williamson, *A Return to Love: Reflections on the Principles of "A Course in Miracles"* (HarperCollins, 1992).

[2] U.S. Census Bureau, *QuickFacts: United States*, n.d., https://www.census.gov/quickfacts/fact/table/US/PST045222.

[3] "Law by the Numbers: New ABA Profile of the Legal Profession," American Bar Association, n.d., https://www.americanbar.org/news/abanews/aba-news-archives/2019/08/profile-of-the-profession-report/.

AVOID THE TEMPTATION OF PURSUING TACTICS OVER STRATEGY

As a reader, you may have already identified very specific questions you would like to have answered, and I encourage you to preview those pages. However, to maximize your results with this book, I encourage you not to skip the initial sections of this book. The mindset you have when implementing video is more important than the technical tools you may be seeking.

A common mistake I have encountered is that, when people are studying someone's success, we tend to observe a person's outcome and the actions we see and come to a conclusion that the success is based solely on the things we can observe. We go on to assign a causal relationship between those two things.

For example, you may watch a YouTuber using a specific camera, background, or similar presentation style in their videos and incorrectly attribute their success to what you have observed. In those instances, we are making the mistake of prioritizing tactics over strategy.

As a result, many of you will be tempted to skip over the content that you will deem as "fluff" in favor of the technical components regarding more sexy topics like, "What camera should I use?" and "How do I get video to look cool?"

Resist this temptation because the actions that make the difference are not usually as obvious. It's not always the tactic or technical tool. Usually, and most of the time with video, it is the perspective they bring to the table that makes the difference. This is the reason why you can find highly successful businesses and law firms that lack sophistication technically experiencing significant success. These organizations prioritize simple strategy over excessive tactical execution. In other words, they do the hard work of thinking about the why so that they can be even more effective with the how. Their ability to have clear strategic thought enables them to focus on the simple but powerful ways they can move their organizations forward.

When we fail to approach the use of video from a strategic perspective first and focus more on the tactical elements, we run the risk of investing significant time, money, and energy perfecting tactics that fail to move us forward. From a practical perspective, this means you have fancy videos but no connection and impact. Your firm's efficiency does not improve, potential clients cannot tell what makes you better or different from your competitors, and your firm remains in the same place while you grow increasingly depleted by failed misaligned efforts to propel your firm forward. So again, I repeat, resist the temptation to prioritize tactics over strategy.

The initial chapters in this book were designed to address the strategic perspective settings you need so that when the technical elements are applied, they are aligned with your desired outcomes and produce the intended results. Keep all the concepts in Part 1 in mind throughout your entire experience of this book.

If this is a journey you are interested in, let's get started.

PART 1

The Essentials

1

The Case for Starting Now

> "The best time to start was yesterday.
> The next best time is now."
>
> —Unknown

I vividly remember the first Facebook Live video I did for my law firm. It was July 21, 2017, the day after my birthday, and I was terrified. I did not have any fancy video equipment or cool gadgets. All I had was my Samsung Galaxy cell phone. But I wanted to share something, and this was the easiest and cheapest way for me to put my message out there. It was a simple way to let people know that I had something that could be of value to them.

I told myself that I would stream the video sometime in the early afternoon, so I went to work getting ready. I put some makeup on and brushed my hair. I agonized over what I would wear and what it would convey and settled on a simple white blouse. I looked in the mirror and looked as good as I could, but still did not feel ready.

It was not that I did not know what I wanted to share. The plan was to say a quick, "Thank you for the birthday messages, and by the way I created these resources you might like. Let me know if you're interested."

But something was gnawing at me.

I paced on the house's first floor, wondering if I should do this. A chorus of questions that I have since become very comfortable with began:

- Is anyone going to watch this?
- Is anyone going to care?
- What are the other lawyers going to think?
- Will they know how desperate I am?
- Will this undermine what I'm trying to build?

The questions continued. But then something disrupted my thoughts. While contemplating my entire life and what the world would think of me, I looked down at my phone. Someone else had started their own Facebook Live, but it wasn't legally related. This Facebook Live was very different from mine. The individual was using the platform to describe her dating life.

Now there are meaningful conversations about the ways people interact and how relationships are developed. This was not one of them. It lacked substance and depth and, to be honest, was quite crass. Yet the young woman had no hesitation when it came to sharing her story.

At this point, you may be wondering, What does this have to do with me as a legal professional exploring video? I am glad you asked. As I observed this Facebook Live, I had an epiphany, and I hope you have one too.

And no, I am not about to suggest that you share the intimate details of your life; far from it.

What I am about to suggest, however, is that we may be overthinking this whole thing—particularly in light of our main objectives when it comes to using videos as legal professionals.

The epiphany that I had and I'm hoping to transfer to you today was more of an internal challenge. I began asking myself, Why I am afraid of showing up in this specific way? What is this hesitation to serve people through videos? Why am I essentially hiding help? People use social media broadly, and videos more specifically, for a host of different purposes. The great irony was that I wanted to use videos to empower others, and there was little reason for me to be as afraid as I found myself that day.

Yet I, like most attorneys and legal professionals, had been somewhat conditioned to operate out of fear. The rhetoric behind much of the innovation that our industry resists often results in being terrified to take allowable risks. However, it was at that moment that I made a decision. I chose to embrace my desire to serve others and resist my reluctance to being seen.

I had to remember that we, as legal professionals, are problem solvers. We are the brave ones, and we are most aligned with our professional values and the integrity of our profession when we embrace opportunities to be strong and courageous. Our clients come to us to bring clarity, and our teams look to us for direction. When we focus solely on our fears, we eclipse the good that can be achieved when we show up whether that be in rooms in person or in virtual spaces. There is no difference.

So, before we jump into the technicalities of video, we must address the most significant obstacles that most attorneys interested in incorporating video face—the overwhelming and paralyzing desire to wait until everything is perfect, and its close counterpart, the compulsion to postpone action until all that can be learned is known and mastered. Most legal professionals are waiting for

- the perfect moment ("I'll start in January because the new year is the *best* time to launch . . ."), or
- the perfect look ("I'll start when I lose those extra 5 pounds . . ."), or
- the perfect equipment ("I'll start when my home studio is built . . .").

Regardless of the reason behind your waiting, there are two things you must realize. First, waiting does not solve any of those problems. As Albert Einstein supposedly said, "Insanity is doing the same thing over and over and expecting different results." You must move past the waiting and take action. Second, there are several individuals with a fraction of the skill, resources, and passion that you have who are changing their firms and the lives of those they serve. And that's the heart of taking action: coming to a place where you understand the cost of your inaction. Let's tackle this head on. I want you to have an aha! moment like mine—minus the random Facebook Live story.

One way to experience this shift in perspective is to address the what-ifs in the room. What are all the crazy things you are scared that could happen to you if you start implementing video in your firm? What are the shame gremlins, as Brené Brown likes to call them, saying to you?[1] A few common what-ifs for attorneys are

- What if I say the wrong thing?
- What if no one watches this?
- What if I look terrible?
- What if I sound like I don't know what I'm doing?

How am I doing so far with the list? I want you to take a few minutes to let the gremlins speak. Don't be scared. You'll be okay. Listen to the questions they are

[1] Brené Brown, *The Power of Vulnerability: Teachings on Authenticity, Connection and Courage* (Sounds True, 2012), audiobook.

asking. Then, I want you to do something I learned from Valorie Burton, a professional development coach.[2]

I want you to write down the questions you hear and answer them.

If your what-ifs by some strange chance were to, in fact, happen, what would you do? Don't dwell on how you'll feel because the truth is, you might feel a bit crummy. Instead, what will you do? What will be your next step? Write these answers out. Give your game plans as much airtime as you gave the what-if gremlins. Determine your plan. So, if you say the wrong thing, how will you correct it? If you are unsure, identify who you will turn to for support. Tell yourself that you will ask for help. This process is a game plan to address your hesitation.

Essentially, these fears can present somewhat legitimate reasons to wait and reflect on things. However, just waiting is not the answer. The answer is to develop a strategy. Underneath the blanket of valid concerns, these gremlins are our attempts to protect ourselves from the vulnerability of creating video. When we wait for perfection before we step out of our comfort zones, we inhibit and delay our progress. There are lessons on the other side of trying that perfection will never help you reach. These lessons require active engagement and commitment from you.

Now, let's keep talking to these what-if creatures. This time, let us chat with the what-if fairies. Yes, we will speak of fairies in this book about lawyer videos. Stay with me.

Since we have given energy and attention to the negative what-ifs, it is only fair and logical that we spend time exploring and developing a clear vision of the positive outcomes that are equally possible.[3] So, turn to the what-if fairies and ask yourself positive what-ifs:

- What if I say the right things?
- What if people do watch my video?
- What if my video looks great (or at least not terrible)?
- What if I sound like I know what I'm doing?

As you address those questions, you may have answers like the following:

- I'll establish myself as a thought leader in my community, which would likely lead to more qualified leads.
- My team will have a library of low-production videos, but those videos will still show them what to do, saving me time.

[2] Valorie Burton, *Successful Women Think Differently* (Harvest House, 2012).

[3] Valorie Burton, *What If It Does Work?*, weekly newsletter, https://valorieburton.com/what-if-it-does-work/.

- I could get a few inquiries about the services I provide.
- I could learn how to do something brand new.
- I could inspire people to take action on issues they should be prioritizing.

Amid your fear, understand that you stand to gain much more than you may have realized initially. Since I'm a few years ahead of you on the video creation journey, I can tell you that the reality is that you'll face a mix of both gremlins and fairies. Embrace the fact that you won't have certainty regarding these things until you act. Once you take your next steps, the weight of the unknown decreases.

But know this: You are well equipped to navigate both. First, you invested in this book. You are not jumping into this unprepared, and you are not alone. The pages of this book will help you identify how you can show up in a way that feels authentic and ethically sound. And because you purchased this book, you will be positioned to have more encounters with positive outcomes.

Next, if you use video the way I describe it in this book, you will have systems that save you time and energy when working with clients and your team. Recording videos can be a tool that continuously creates value even if you are not recording new videos every day.

Legal professionals often fail to capitalize on the opportunities to use tools like video because we lose sight of our value and purpose. I doubt that you are creating videos to stroke your ego. You are probably doing it to provide value and insight to your team, clients, and potential leads. You are creating an avenue for your audience to realize that help is near.

Video, in this form then, is not about you, even if you are the subject or the main character. It is about the impact your video will have on the intended audience. It is about how your team members will receive more comprehensive training because of your videos. It is about how your potential clients will have a more precise understanding of your process and more accurate expectations set by you instead of the latest trending legal drama.

In essence, you desire to serve people. If you keep this desire to help your community and your team at the forefront of your mind, you will find the courage to start.

COVID-19 AND THE PANDEMIC THAT TAUGHT US THE VALUE OF VIDEO

This is a special time in our history. Before the 2020 coronavirus pandemic, many legal practitioners probably felt that video as a strategic tool had little place in the legal industry. However, when lives were at stake, change came. The most formal proceedings, like trials, were wholly conducted virtually. The pandemic forced us to consider how routine events like the notarization of estate planning and real estate documents could be completed with technology. Video proved capable of rising to the challenge.

Wyzowl, a global leader in creating animated videos for companies worldwide, has produced an annual report, *The State of Video Marketing*.[4] This report is based on data collected from companies and consumers to measure trends in video marketing. Their findings shed significant light on how both consumers and marketers engage with video as society emerges from the effects of the pandemic.

In "Video Marketing Statistics," Wyzowl found that 90 percent of consumers said videos helped them make buying decisions.[5] Seventy-seven percent of people said that a video convinced them to buy software or download an application based on a video they watched.[6] Seventy-three percent of the consumers surveyed preferred to watch a short video to learn about a product or service instead of consuming information via another medium.[7]

Additionally, 43 percent of the marketers who participated recognized the pressure COVID brought and said that video became necessary due to challenges arising from the pandemic.[8] Eighty-six percent of businesses used video marketing as a tool to support their marketing efforts.[9] Finally, when it comes to sharing information, consumers were twice as likely to share video content over other forms of content (images and text alone).[10] For my logical lawyer comrades, the numbers are there. The world is primed for the continued emergence of video in every industry and field—including law.

---

[4] "Video Marketing Statistics," *Wyzowl*, https://www.wyzowl.com/video-marketing-statistics/.

[5] "Video Marketing Statistics," *Wyzowl*, https://www.wyzowl.com/video-marketing-statistics/.

[6] "7 Video Marketing Statistics That Will Blow Your Mind," *Wyzowl*, 2023, https://www.wyzowl.com/amazing-video-marketing-statistics/#:~:text=A%20slightly%20smaller%20%E2%80%93%20but%20still,app%20by%20watching%20a%20video.&text=The%20takeaway%20here%3A%20if%20you,smart%20way%20to%20do%20it!.

[7] "The Ultimate List of Marketing Statistics for 2024," *Hubspot* (blog), https://www.hubspot.com/marketing-statistics

[8] "Video Marketing Statistics 2022," *Wyzowl*, https://www.wyzowl.com/sovm-results-2022/.

[9] Jeanne Melvin, "10 Video Statistics That Will Blow Your Mind," *Wyzowl*, May 17, 2022, https://www.wyzowl.com/amazing-video-marketing-statistics/.

[10] "The power of video content in 15 statistics," *Semantix*, https://www.semantix.com/resources/blog/the-power-of-video.

WHAT'S AT STAKE?

When I reflect on where I started, I am so glad I started imperfectly, and you can start imperfectly too. It is not too late. When I introduce the idea of recording videos to the lawyers I have coached and the audiences I speak to, I often recommend finding your favorite YouTubers and exploring how they started. Try to scroll back to their earliest videos to see what things looked like for them at the beginning. An exercise like this can be a reminder to you that everyone must start somewhere, and often that somewhere is not the smoothest.

If I had waited until I understood how to create videos perfectly and tried to do everything the way the "experts" did, I would never have started. I would have instead cycled repeatedly in my head. I would have deceived myself into believing that my videos were not valuable. And the thousands of individuals who have now found the videos I created about navigating our industry would not have had access to this information.

Who is waiting for you to start? Which clients struggle to find you and will continue to struggle as you delay your start? Are they waiting for your perfect video, or are they ready for the value you provide, even if it does not contain all the bells and whistles it could?

When you are in the thick of building your business and life, it is sometimes easy to get so caught up that the urgency of the moment is lost on you. The same can be said when it comes to implementing video in your firm.

When I think about our relationship with time, I think of an analogy from a speaker I know. He described the concept of stagnancy in a way that has never left me. One Sunday morning, he asked his audience something along these lines: "You know those conveyor belts that objects are placed on? Imagine one with toys on it heading toward a furnace.

"As the object stays still, it may feel safe, it may feel protected, but the truth is that place of rest and comfort it seems to enjoy is moving it toward destruction. That is essentially our lives."

Here's the point: Stagnancy may feel comfortable and safe, but it is not. It moves us toward danger and keeps us away from our goals. If you are someone seriously considering video, time is steadily drifting away as you wait to act.

When you fail to take that first step, you stay stagnant. You lose the opportunity to establish yourself as a thought leader in your space during this time. You risk becoming irrelevant and disconnected from people who would benefit from your services.

But still I understand. Ultimately, there are many legitimate reasons to wait:

- You can wait until you have the right camera.
- You can wait until you have grown your following.
- You can wait until you lose a few more pounds.
- You can wait until your office is perfect.

Yes, technically, you can wait, but there is a cost to that decision. You cannot afford to mull over how to create the perfect shot and buy the ideal tool—especially if you are not trying to become a professional videographer. The truth is that you have much more to gain when you act than to lose when you choose to wait.

You also cannot afford to keep deceiving yourself by calling your research action. Most of the time that is not what it is. It is procrastination. The irony is that some of the things you are waiting to achieve or experience before you implement video will happen faster *if* you implement video. The things you are wondering will be discovered in your forward progress.

In the next section of this book, we will tackle one of the most significant sources of fear and hence delay for attorneys interested in using video in their firms: ethics.

2

Ethical Considerations for Using Video

As a baby lawyer, I remember sitting in the conference room in the Harris County Public Defender's Office with about 10 other baby attorneys. This was a meeting for newer attorneys who needed mentorship, and one of our mentors was sharing his three cardinal rules for those entering the legal profession.

He stood at the front of the room and said with his friendly, but booming voice, "Rule number one: Don't lose your bar card." I looked around the room and noticed that we all felt comfortable with that rule. After three gruelling years of tedious texts and tough professors, followed by a three-day examination that challenged our mental fortitude, that sounded about right.

He continued, "Rule number two: Don't lose your bar card." I began to sense a pattern, but to my surprise, rule number three was different. He concluded, "Rule number three: Don't break rules one and two."

Ethics in the legal industry, while a common conversation topic, seems to be surrounded by fear. I think back to my professional responsibility class in law school; that professor struck a deep fear in his students regarding how easy it is to lose your license, a fear that continued after graduation.

In our profession, it seems we often learn more about what not to do than what we can and are expected to do. Additionally, technological enhancements are rarely considered during these conversations. The result? Little to no guidance on how to effectively practice and navigate an increasingly technological society.

After the COVID-19 pandemic, however, that should no longer be the case. Even if we were reluctant as an industry to embrace the opportunities technological advancements present us as leaders in our communities, the events of 2020 and beyond require that serious attention be given to the ethical implications for evolving technological enhancements broadly and with video and other communications media specifically.

In addressing this within the context of implementing video in a firm, it's important to note that our industry's fear-based approach to ethical considerations may have hindered some of the objectives it intends to achieve. In other words, attorneys can become so riddled with fear regarding ethical violations that they find themselves reluctant to change even if some of those apprehensions are not warranted and undermine other ethical considerations. This reluctance then causes many attorneys to miss out on opportunities for greater efficiency and communication, which would ultimately benefit our clients.

So now that you have decided to start implementing video, this section of the book attempts to bridge that gap between our well-warranted fear and the opportunities for innovation and creative connection. I want us to tackle the gremlin that says, "You are going to make a video and lose your license." We will do this by examining the most relevant provisions of the American Bar Association's (ABA) Model Rules of Professional Conduct and a few ABA formal opinions to understand what you can do, what you cannot do, and what you should do as leaders in society and those providing zealous representation. The following are the provisions we will explore:

1. Rule 1.1: Competence
2. Rule 1.4: Communications
3. Rule 1.6: Confidentiality of Information
4. Rule 7.1: Communications Concerning a Lawyer's Services
5. Rule 7.2: Communications Concerning a Lawyer's Services: Specific Rules
6. Rule 7.3: Solicitation of Clients

A CAVEAT BEFORE WE CONTINUE

Before we unpack what these rules say, some legal professionals may wonder whether the ABA Model Rules have any direct relevance to them in their own jurisdiction, since they are not binding on any practitioner unless their state has adopted the rule. However, every state has adopted ethics rules that are modeled on or at least influenced by the ABA Model Rules. Each state has also made changes to the model rules: how and to what extent they have adopted them also vary. Therefore, the guidance we provide in this book is subject to your jurisdiction's rules.

Let's begin our conversation examining a few of the things we *must do* under the ABA's model rules. When we start the conversation examining what we have to do before examining what we cannot do, we adopt a mindset that helps us think expansively about what is possible and operate from the leadership role society tends to naturally and reasonably expect from us.

ABA MODEL RULE 1.1: COMPETENCE

Model Rule 1.1 states, "A lawyer shall provide **competent representation** to a client. Competent representation requires the **legal knowledge, skill, thoroughness and preparation reasonably necessary for the representation**. [emphasis added][1]

On its face, this rule appears to address an attorney's duty as it relates to the substantive requirements of knowledge—understanding the law, preparing to defend positions, and so forth. However, in 2012, the ABA added a comment to this rule that clarifies how Model Rule 1.1 imposes a broader duty beyond the substantive legal knowledge attorneys are trained in.

Comment [8] of Rule 1.1 says, "To maintain the requisite knowledge and skill, *a lawyer should keep abreast of changes in the* **law and its practice**, **including the benefits and risks associated with relevant technology**, engage in continuing study and education and comply with all continuing legal education requirements to which the lawyer is subject" [emphasis added in bold and italic].[2]

This comment explicitly sets out the standard for technological competence that is implied by the text of Model Rule 1.1. As of March 2022, 40 states have adopted this specific rule and comment. That means most of the attorneys in this country have an underlying duty to comply with the various components of this rule.[3]

---

[1] "Model Rule 1.1: Competence, Comment [8]," American Bar Association, 2016, p. 19, https://www.americanbar.org/content/dam/aba/administrative/professional_responsibility/mrpc1-1-comment-8.pdf.

[2] Ibid.

[3] "Model Rule 1.1: Competence, Comment [8]," American Bar Association, 2016, https://www.americanbar.org/content/dam/aba/administrative/professional_responsibility/mrpc1-1-comment-8.pdf.

The term "relevant technology" is not explicitly defined; however, the preceding clause incorporates "the law and its practice." Because video use in conferencing and marketing impacts law practice, many practitioners and bar associations believe video falls within the purview of relevant technology.[4] In complying with this rule, an attorney should, therefore, understand the benefits and risks associated with video use.

This book was created on the premise that the benefits typically outweigh the risks, and these benefits are highlighted throughout, but can be summarized into five main ideas:

- Clarity. Video can help you explain concepts more clearly.
- Convenience. Video can make it easier for you to connect with your clients, your team, and other people in your industry or market.
- Access. Video can be accessed in a wide variety of ways.
- Scalability. Video can allow you to reach more people with greater ease—if you desire to do so.
- Engagement. Video can help people engage with you and the information you provide in a way that helps them experience more fully understand what you are communicating.

As you work through this book, you will see how powerful these benefits can be. They can transform things for you, your team, and your clients. However, risks do in fact exist and we need to be aware of those to comply with this rule and to optimize our impact.

Many of the risks associated with video use are related to the subsequent model rules we will discuss; however, they can be packaged into two categories:

- Security. The positive increase of accessibility comes with increased risks that bad faith actors can access and encounter information via video.
- Confidentiality. With our duty of confidentiality, attorneys using video must be intentional about maintaining the security of our clients' data addressed, included or exchanged via video.

It is interesting to note that the very medium many practitioners are scared to use is in fact being used to help attorneys and legal professionals comply with this

---

[4] Jennifer Anderson, "A Lawyer's Duty of Technological Competence," *InfoTrack* (blog), February 3, 2022, https://www.infotrack.com/blog/duty-of-technological-competence/; see also Constangy, Brooks, Smith & Prophete LLP, "California Bar Requires Attorneys to Embrace Technology," *JD Supra*, March 30, 2021, https://www.jdsupra.com/legalnews/california-bar-requires-attorneys-to-5727418/.

requirement by creating videos and posting them on bar websites and social media platforms like YouTube.[5]

The subsequent model rules will help us unpack these concerns in greater detail.

ABA MODEL RULE 1.4: COMMUNICATIONS[6]

Another rule that speaks to what we must do is Model Rule 1.4 on communications. Specifically, it reads, "A lawyer shall:

1. promptly inform the client of any decision or circumstance with respect to which the client's informed consent, as defined in Rule 1.0(e), is required by these Rules;
2. reasonably consult with the client about the means by which the client's objectives are to be accomplished;
3. keep the client reasonably informed about the status of the matter;
4. promptly comply with reasonable requests for information; and
5. consult with the client about any relevant limitation on the lawyer's conduct when the lawyer knows that the client expects assistance not permitted by the Rules of Professional Conduct or other law.

(b) A lawyer shall explain a matter to the extent reasonably necessary to permit the client to make informed decisions regarding the representation."[7]

I incorporate Model Rule 1.4 into this discussion because video provides unique opportunities to comply with this rule and this specific rule has been widely adopted across the United States. Essentially, Model Rule 1.4 speaks to the necessity of attorneys to stay in communication with clients. As we learned during

[5] Dan Kittay, "(Safely) Using All the Tools in the Toolbox: Bars Help Members Gain Technological Competence," *Bar Leader* 43, no. 3 (January-February 2019), https://www.americanbar.org/groups/bar_services/publications/bar_leader/2018_19/january-february/safely-using-all-the-tools-in-the-toolbox-bars-help-members-gain-technological-competence/.

[6] "Model Rule 1.4: Communications," American Bar Association, https://www.americanbar.org/groups/professional_responsibility/publications/model_rules_of_professional_conduct/rule_1_4_communications/.

[7] Ibid.

the pandemic, this duty still exists even when it is inconvenient or during a crisis.[8] However, lawyers should not only use video in times of distress. Video can help attorneys stay connected throughout representations by making it easier to communicate and meet via video conferencing.

And consider this: Could this duty to communicate be achieved using prerecorded videos as well? When there are portions of the representation that an attorney reasonably anticipates will come up, what's stopping the attorney from developing prerecorded content that can be released to clients over the course of the representation that keeps "the client reasonably informed about the status of the matter"?[9] That is just one example of using video to comply with the ethical requirement of communication.

ABA MODEL RULE 1.6: CONFIDENTIALITY OF INFORMATION[10]

Model Rule 1.6: Confidentiality of Information is fundamental to the legal profession and can be expressed as one of our "can't do" rules. Unlike the previous model rules explored, this rule poses one of the most significant risks associated with video for attorneys. Model Rule 1.6, paragraph (c) states, "A lawyer shall make reasonable efforts to prevent the inadvertent or unauthorized disclosure of, or unauthorized access to, information relating to the representation of a client."[11]

In this regard, legal professionals must take precautions to protect the client's information. The language here also notes mistakes that could potentially occur. As an attorney incorporating video conferring into your practice, you must take *reasonable* steps to avoid accidents. But first, we must address what constitutes reasonable efforts. We must also explore what could create the inadvertent or unauthorized disclosure of information. Paragraph 18 of the comment further elaborates on this point.

---

[8] "Ethics in the COVID-19 Pandemic," State Bar of Michigan, https://www.michbar.org/opinions/ethics/COVID-19.

[9] "Model Rule 1.4: Communications," paragraph (a), parts 3 and 4, American Bar Association, https://www.americanbar.org/groups/professional_responsibility/publications/model_rules_of_professional_conduct/rule_1_4_communications/.

[10] "Model Rule 1.6: Confidentiality of Information," American Bar Association, https://www.americanbar.org/groups/professional_responsibility/publications/model_rules_of_professional_conduct/rule_1_6_confidentiality_of_information/.

[11] Ibid.

Paragraph 18 helps us understand that "the unauthorized access to, or the inadvertent or unauthorized disclosure of information relating to the representation of a client does not constitute a violation of paragraph (c) if the lawyer has made reasonable efforts to prevent the access or disclosure."[12] The comment continues by outlining the following nonexclusive factors to be considered when trying to figure out whether the attorney's efforts are reasonable:

- "the sensitivity of the information,
- the likelihood of disclosure if additional safeguards are not employed,
- the cost of employing additional safeguards,
- the difficulty of implementing the safeguards,
- the extent to which the safeguards adversely affect the lawyer's ability to represent clients."[13]

In Formal Opinion 477R, the ABA's Standing Committee on Ethics and Professional Responsibility further explained that there are not any specific security requirements.[14] The committee shared that attorneys should instead put forth on "a fact-specific approach" to meeting these obligations.[15]

Putting it all together, we must keep both the duty to communicate and the duty to maintain confidentiality at the forefront of selecting the methods we use to communicate with our clients. We want to select communication methods based on our understanding of the risks and benefits of communication technology and the information being communicated. A failure to adequately understand and apply such knowledge has the potential to be viewed as a failure of duty on the attorney's part. With this ethical foundation, let's consider what can be done to meet these rules.

Controlling Location

As you explore this mode of communication with your clients, there are several steps you can take to reduce the risks associated with video and handling

[12] "Model Rule 1.6 – Comment," American Bar Association, https://www.americanbar.org/groups/professional_responsibility/publications/model_rules_of_professional_conduct/rule_1_6_confidentiality_of_information/comment_on_rule_1_6/#:~:text=%5B18%5D%20Paragraph%20(c),the%20client%20or%20who%20are.

[13] Ibid.

[14] "ABA Formal Opinion 477," American Bar Association, https://www.americanbar.org/content/dam/aba/administrative/professional_responsibility/ethics-opinions/aba-formal-opinion-477.pdf.

[15] Ibid.

confidential information during conferences. To start, explore your physical location. Before participating in a video conference related to representation or potential representation where participants may share confidential information, find a quiet and secure space. The site you select should not be in a public or high-traffic area where others will have the ability to hear what is discussed. As an extra precaution, consider using headphones or earbuds. Although headphones will not impact the words you speak, you will still be reducing the chances of accidentally disclosing confidential information.

Additionally, in a secure space, you will decrease the risks of a smart device picking up on your conversation because only one side of the conversation would be audible. And speaking of smart devices, you should not overlook the risks associated with those tools.[16] These devices are designed to remain sensitive to hearing all the sounds within their environments.[17] When these devices hear, "Hello, Siri" or "Alexa" or any other similar voice-activated prompts or sounds , they start recording.[18] Therefore, be careful when using recording near smart devices. Some states even recommend turning off the listening functions when discussing client matters.[19] This means paying attention to your phones, smart watches, stand-alone devices, and other smart tools that may have these voice-activated capabilities. In taking these steps, you are addressing the concerns of Model Rule 1.6.

Managing Access

After securing your physical location from risk, you need to secure your virtual location. If you want to improve your management in this area, look to understanding the existing software or virtual platform. Selecting software with security in mind is part of meeting our ethical responsibilities.[20]

Typical video conferencing tools provide a few different ways to authenticate or limit access to your conference call. In some instances, you may find that you

---

[16] Ibid.

[17] Brett Taylor and Scot Ganow, "Smart Devices: Convenient, Helpful, Fun. Oh Yeah, and Possibly Breaching Confidentiality," *Mondaq* (April 18, 2022), https://www.mondaq.com/unitedstates/privacy-protection/1184060/smart-devices-convenient-helpful-fun-oh-yeah-and-possibly-breaching-confidentiality.

[18] Ibid.

[19] Jennifer Anderson, "A Lawyer's Duty of Technological Competence. *InfoTrack* (blog), February 3, 2022, https://www.infotrack.com/blog/duty-of-technological-competence/.

[20] Constancy, Brooks, Smith & Prophete LLP, "California Bar Requires Attorneys to Embrace Technology," *JD Supra*, March 30, 2021, https://www.jdsupra.com/legalnews/california-bar-requires-attorneys-to-5727418/.

can restrict access by way of requiring a passcode.[21] Best practices for using passcodes and passwords is to change them often and use only strong passwords.[22] Most software will actually help develop new passcodes each time you use the software. When using this approach, do not share your passcodes on public or social forums. Send the codes to the invited participants directly.

You can also explore limiting access to your video conference to people who are registered or authenticated users.[23] In many cases, the authentication is completed using your email address. You can also utilize virtual waiting rooms that allow you to let people enter your virtual meeting spaces manually.[24] If you see a name that you are not familiar with in the waiting room, do not allow that person into your conference room.

Along those same lines, consider updating your security settings that allow you to limit the regions where your participants may be located. Some platforms allow you to easily specify the regions where your participants are joining from, which can help further restrict who can access the call. Failure to take these precautions can leave your meeting vulnerable to attacks from unauthorized individuals without the passcodes or from regions outside of your geographical scope. These individuals may then have access to confidential information or may be participating in the phenomenon called Zoombombing.

In Zoombombing, someone uninvited joins a group for the purposes of disrupting the virtual gathering by sharing disturbing or inappropriate content.[25] In 2022, Harris County courts were the victims of such activity, but were able to resume proceedings without needing to cancel or reschedule.[26] That being said, Zoombombing still occurs, but has significantly decreased.[27] Companies like

---

[21] Pennsylvania Bar Association Committee on Legal Ethics and Professional Responsibility, *Formal Opinion 2020-300* (Pennsylvania Bar Association, 2020.)

[22] "ABA Formal Opinion 498," American Bar Association, https://www.americanbar.org/content/dam/aba/administrative/professional_responsibility/aba-formal-opinion-498.pdf.

[23] Pennsylvania Bar Association Committee on Legal Ethics and Professional Responsibility *Formal Opinion 2020-300* (Pennsylvania Bar Association, 2020).

[24] Ibid.

[25] "What Is Zoom Bombing?," Delgado Community College, https://www.dcc.edu/administration/offices/information-technology/zoom/zoom-bombing.aspx

[26] Adam Zuvanich, "Harris County Court 'Zoom Bombed' with Explicit Images; Sheriff's Office Investigating," *Houston Public Media*, December 14, 2022, https://www.houstonpublicmedia.org/articles/news/harris-county/2022/12/14/439498/harris-county-court-zoom-bomb-explicit-images/.

[27] Shira Ovide, "Remember Zoom-Bombing? This Is How Zoom Tamed Meeting Instructions," *Washington Post*, January 24, 2023, https://www.washingtonpost.com/technology/2023/01/24/zoom-bombing-prevention-tips/.

Zoom have faced hefty settlement costs in the past due to inadequate security features that made it easier for these violations to occur. To avoid additional legal liability, most video conferencing providers have improved the security features on their platforms to avoid such recurrences.[28]

When thinking about managing access during video conferences, you should include managing screen-sharing options. Screen sharing increases the risk of accidentally sharing clients' confidential information with unauthorized people. To protect against this risk, first, limit who can share their screen during a meeting. Doing this, particularly with your team, can protect against a team member accidentally sharing information from the firm.

Next, encourage team members to minimize or close inactive files during video conferences. With one accidental click, someone may share the wrong window, and information is accidentally shared. If windows are not up or open in the background, the chances that confidential information is shared significantly diminishes. Finally, some video conferencing tools allow you to limit your screen sharing to specific windows or tabs. Check to see if this feature is available and use it when it is.

Another helpful tool is ensuring that the links to the virtual rooms between meetings differ. In other words, use different meeting links for each meeting. This is especially important when you have back-to-back meetings that involve separate confidential content. If you do not create these different meeting links, another participant or client from a different representation could accidentally join a meeting for another client and gain access to confidential information.

Recording, Storing, and Sharing Video and Transcripts

If you choose to use video to communicate with clients, you may also have the option to record and store the video and transcripts. How you handle these recordings may fall within the parameters of ethical obligations. The discussion of virtual practices in ABA Formal Opinion 498 advises that "any recordings or transcripts should be secured."[29] Formal Opinion 498 also notes, "If the platform will be recording conversations with the client, it is inadvisable to do so without

---

[28] Ibid. See also Esquire Deposition Solutions, "Make Your Zoom Meeting as Secure as Possible," *JD Supra*, February 10, 2021, https://www.jdsupra.com/legalnews/make-your-zoom-meeting-as-secure-as-2693441/.

[29] "ABA Formal Opinion 498," American Bar Association, https://www.americanbar.org/content/dam/aba/administrative/professional_responsibility/aba-formal-opinion-498.pdf.

client consent, but lawyers should consult the professional conduct rules, ethics opinions, and laws of the applicable jurisdiction."[30] For example, New York amended its *New York Rules of Professional Conduct* to include video recordings in the expansion of what may need to be stored as an electronic communications.[31] The admissibility of the video recording of a proceeding is a topic that is beyond the scope of this book, but the litigation in this area is something to keep an eye on.[32]

All the strategies described help attorneys comply with Rule 1.6(c), the duty to protect client information.[33] However, it can be helpful to compile the firm's practices for protecting client information into firm policies and procedures that are taught to members of your team. The policies you implement should align with the best practices outlined by the software providers.

Finally, if you are creating and sharing prerecorded material, remember to ensure that confidential information is not accidentally recorded and accessed by the wrong parties. These safety measures may include, for example, only recording the relevant portions of your screen, blurring out confidential or personal information, or password-protecting access to the recordings. These various measures show that you understand the risks and that you are actively protecting against them.

ETHICAL CONSIDERATIONS FOR VIDEO MARKETING

The next few model rules we will examine focus on attorney advertising, so before we continue looking at those rules, let's take a moment to unpack the historical development of this area to understand the essence of these regulations. Restrictions on how attorneys market their practice date back to the early 1900s and were seen as accomplishing two primary purposes: (1) maintaining the integrity and

---

[30] Ibid.

[31] *Social Media Ethics Guidelines of the Commercial and Federal Litigation Section of the New York State Bar Association* (New York State Bar Association, amended June 10, 2022, release date June 18, 2022), https://nysba.org/app/uploads/2022/07/Rules-of-Professional-Conduct-as-amended-6.10.2022-20220701.pdf.

[32] Philip Zisook, "Attorneys Beware: Zoom Depositions Are Likely Inadmissible," *Law360* (June 21, 2021), https://www.law360.com/articles/1395474/attorneys-beware-zoom-depositions-are-likely-inadmissible.

[33] Esquire Deposition Solutions LLC, "Make Your Zoom Meeting as Secure as Possible," *JD Supra*, February 10, 2021, https://www.jdsupra.com/legalnews/make-your-zoom-meeting-as-secure-as-2693441/.

professionalism of the practice of law[34] and (2) protecting consumers from being tricked by the complex narratives woven together by attorneys.[35]

These underlying principles were used as a justification for states imposing total bans on attorney advertisements until the 1977 landmark United States Supreme Court decision in *Bates* v. *State Bar of Arizona*.[36] This case involved two lawyers challenging Arizona's total prohibition on attorney advertisements. For the first time, the Supreme Court held that attorney advertising was constitutionally protected commercial speech under the First Amendment. The holding in *Bates* changed the game and established that attorneys had certain First Amendment freedom of speech protections.

Writing the majority opinion of the court, Justice Harry A. Blackmun stated, "In holding that advertising by attorneys may not be subjected to blanket suppression, and that the advertisement at issue is protected, we, of course, do not hold that states may not regulate advertising by attorneys in any way."[37] In other words, even though the Court was expanding attorneys' opportunities to advertise, they carved out room to allow the states to regulate that advertising. This clarification highlighted a tension between exercising commercial freedom of speech for attorneys in advertising and a state's right to regulate such speech. This tension still exists today and forms the basis for much of what we must consider when creating videos for marketing.

Interestingly, many of the same concerns the attorneys pointed out to the court in *Bates* v. *State Bar of Arizona* remain relevant today. The attorneys for the lawyers noted in their appellate brief that advertising was a way of communicating information to clients to empower them to make better decisions. The same can be said for attorneys employing video to connect with prospective clients today. Effective marketing should make it easier for potential clients to understand that you are an option for them as they seek legal counsel or services.

In our treatment of legal marketing, we will deal with three primary rules: Model Rule 7.1 addresses the prohibition of false or misleading communications about a lawyer's services, Model Rule 7.2 provides specific regulations regarding

---

[34] Shaheen P. Adibi, "Why Was Lawyer Advertising Banned? Exploring the Historical Restrictions," *Web Upon*, April 26, 2024, https://webupon.com/blog/why-was-lawyer-advertising-banned/#:~:text=Origins%20of%20Advertising%20Restrictions&text=At%20the%20turn%20of%20the,considered%20demeaning%20to%20the%20profession.

[35] "History of Attorney Advertising," *Socially Awkward*, https://sociallyawkwardlaw.com/attorney-advertising-regulation/history-of-attorney-advertising/.

[36] Bates v. State Bar of Arizona, Oyez, https://www.oyez.org/cases/1976/76-316.

[37] Ibid.

advertising communications, and Model Rule 7.3 regulates attorney solicitation of clients, which occurs when a lawyer or law firm initiates a communication with a person known to need legal services in a particular legal matter and offers to provide legal services for that matter.

ABA MODEL RULE 7.1 COMMUNICATIONS CONCERNING A LAWYER'S SERVICES

Every state has adopted some version of ABA Model Rule 7.1, which states, "A lawyer shall not make a **false or misleading communication about the lawyer or the lawyer's services**. A communication is false or misleading if it contains a material misrepresentation of fact or law, or omits a fact necessary to make the statement considered as a whole not materially misleading." [emphasis added].[38]

Model Rule 7.1's text appears straightforward enough, but there are a few critical elements to consider when developing content for your marketing videos. Now the most prominent aspect of this rule seems to be prohibiting false or misleading communication. Still, the ABA provides even greater insight by defining false or misleading "as a material misrepresentation of fact or law, **or** [something that] omits a fact necessary to make the statement considered as a whole not materially misleading."

This rule provides insight regarding what we should aim to achieve in our marketing and that is truthfulness. Essentially, we must ensure our videos tell the truth. Comment [1] to Model Rule 7.1 further explains, "This Rule governs all communications about a lawyer's services, including advertising. Whatever means are used to make a lawyer's services known, the statement about them must be truthful."[39] In other words, resist the temptation to stretch the truth to grow in popularity. That seems simple enough, but this rule has more for you to consider.

Your communications in any advertising, including advertising through video, should not be misleading. It's not enough to tell the truth. If there is a substantial likelihood that a reasonable person would be led to believe something that is not factually true based on what you've said in your videos, you are violating Model

---

[38] "Model Rule 7.1: Communication Concerning a Lawyer's Services," American Bar Association, https://www.americanbar.org/groups/professional_responsibility/publications/model_rules_of_professional_conduct/rule_7_1_communication_concerning_a_lawyer_s_services/; see also William Hornsby, "Attorney Advertising: The Errors of Your Omissions," *Attorney at Work*, September 16, 2020, https://www.attorneyatwork.com/the-errors-of-your-omissions-attorney-advertising/.

[39] "Comment on Rule 7.1," American Bar Association, https://www.americanbar.org/groups/professional_responsibility/publications/model_rules_of_professional_conduct/rule_7_1_communication_concerning_a_lawyer_s_services/comment_on_rule_7_1/.

Rule 7.1. This is also the case if you leave information out that would lead a reasonable person to conclude that your video's content is false. As a result, make sure that your communication is intentional and precise. This is one reason why preparation is so critical as you market yourself and your firm's services through video.

Even though every state has adopted a version of Model Rule 7.1, what constitutes a violation varies greatly from jurisdiction to jurisdiction. The following examples are developed from actual attorney advertisements (some video and some nonvideo) that were deemed misleading:

- Videos generated by artificial intelligence (AI) that include celebrities who appear to be former clients or associates of the law firm[40]
- Videos on social media that claim that your firm has a certain number of years of experience but fail to mention that this number was derived by adding up and combining everyone's years of experience[41]
- Videos that describe past successes without providing enough information about the nature and details of the case to help the prospective client accurately understand the results[42]

One area where lawyers often need to be careful when advertising is communicating results you have had or may have in representing someone. Video content that promises specific definitive results for clients, for example, "I will get you money for your home," where specific outcomes cannot be guaranteed, will likely violate this rule in most jurisdictions.[43] The expectations you set in your video advertising must be realistic. Tell your audience directly that you cannot guarantee a specific result. And, when possible, use disclaimers. We will unpack when it is necessary and appropriate to use disclaimers, and how to use them soon, but for now, remember that disclaimers help you and the viewer and may also be required by ethics rule.

[40] Michael E. McCabe Jr., "Lawyer Who Photoshopped Self into Celebrity Photos Posted on Firm Website Suspended for Deceptive Advertising," McCabe/Ali LLP, n.d., https://ipethicslaw.com/lawyer-who-photoshopped-self-into-celebrity-photos-posted-on-website-wins-turkey-of-month-award/; California State Bar, "Opinion with Former Attorney Photoshopping Herself into Images with Other Celebrities," Members.calbar, n.d., https://members.calbar.ca.gov/courtDocs/13-O-13838-2.pdf.

[41] William Hornsby, "Can I Say That? The Importance of Avoiding False or Misleading Advertisements: Let's Unpack ABA Model Rule 7.1," *Attorney at Work*, September 11, 2019, www.attorneyatwork.com/can-i-say-that-the-importance-of-avoiding-false-or-misleading-advertisements/.

[42] Ibid.

[43] R. Regul. Fl. Bar 4-7.13, as amended May 30, 2024, *CaseText*, https://casetext.com/rule/florida-court-rules/rules-regulating-the-florida-bar/chapter-4-rules-of-professional-conduct-preamble-a-lawyers-responsibilities/rule-4-7-information-about-legal-services/rule-4-713-deceptive-and-inherently-misleading-advertisements#:~:text=Bar%204%2D7.13,-Download&text=A%20lawyer%20may%20not%20engage,Deceptive%20and%20Inherently%20Misleading%20Advertisements.

As you will see, your marketing should be building trust. Misstated expectations erode that trust and hurt your ability to build trust effectively with potential clients. Beyond the ethical obligations that most state supreme courts impose, this is just healthy business building.[44]

ABA MODEL RULE 7.2: COMMUNICATIONS CONCERNING A LAWYER'S SERVICES: SPECIFICS RULES

The next relevant rule, Model Rule 7.2, addresses specific issues in attorney communications regarding their services. For our reference, the exact text of the rule states the following:

(a) A lawyer may communicate information regarding the lawyer's services through any media.
(b) A lawyer shall not compensate, give or promise anything of value to a person for recommending the lawyer's services except that a lawyer may:
   (1) pay the reasonable costs of advertisements or communications permitted by this Rule;
   (2) pay the usual charges of a legal service plan or a not-for-profit or qualified lawyer referral service;
   (3) pay for a law practice in accordance with Rule 1.17;
   (4) refer clients to another lawyer or a nonlawyer professional pursuant to an agreement not otherwise prohibited under these Rules that provides for the other person to refer clients or customers to the lawyer, if:
      (i) the reciprocal referral agreement is not exclusive; and
      (ii) the client is informed of the existence and nature of the agreement; and
   (5) give nominal gifts as an appreciation that are neither intended nor reasonably expected to be a form of compensation for recommending a lawyer's service.
(c) A lawyer shall not state or imply that a lawyer is certified as a specialist in a particular field of law unless:
   (1) the lawyer has been certified as a specialist by an organization that an appropriate authority has approved of the state or the District of Columbia or a U.S. Territory or that has been accredited by the American Bar Association; and

[44] For your viewing pleasure, if you're interested in a few laughs, check out this compilation of attorney advertising videos: https://esplinweight.com/worst-law-firm-commercials/.

(2) the name of the certifying organization is identified in the communication.

(d) Any communication made under this Rule must include the name and contact information of at least one lawyer or law firm responsible for its content.'[45]

Let's look at each part of this rule and its implications for video creation. Model Rule 7.2(a) establishes that attorneys can use any media for advertising their services. This is excellent news for you reading this book because we are talking about using video on various platforms to connect and communicate with potential clients. Comment [1] to Model Rule 7.2 explains the type of information that a lawyer or firm can share, and it is broad. It includes the names of clients regularly represented, how fees are determined, contact information, "and other information that might invite the attention of those seeking legal assistance."[46] The word "invite" in this comment is particularly valuable because it aligns with what marketing and advertising are expected to do.

Model Rule 7.2, paragraph (b) describes limitations on paying others to recommend a lawyer. Generally, lawyers are not allowed to pay other people to recommend their work, so you could not, for example, provide payment to clients for doing testimonials or case study videos with you unless it is a "reasonable cost of advertising" and in those instances it must be disclosed as a paid testimonial. This would violate the model rules and the rules adopted or modified by most local jurisdictions. This means you have to wow your clients and develop relationships that make people raving fans. You want them to participate in these activities willingly.

Can You Pay for Recommendation Videos?

Another essential point to keep in mind as you create your marketing videos is understanding whether your videos are asking for a recommendation. Comment [2] says that you have a recommendation if the communication "endorses or vouches for a lawyer's credentials, abilities, competence, character, or other

[45] "Rule 7.2: Communications Concerning a Lawyer's Services: Specific Rules," American Bar Association, https://www.americanbar.org/groups/professional_responsibility/publications/model_rules_of_professional_conduct/rule_7_2_advertising/.

[46] "Comment on Rule 7.2: Communications Concerning a Lawyer's Services: Specific Rules," American Bar Association, https://www.americanbar.org/groups/professional_responsibility/publications/model_rules_of_professional_conduct/rule_7_2_advertising/comment_on_rule_7_2/.

professional qualities." Note that this is not saying that you cannot have recommendations. It says that you should not *pay* for recommendations. On the other hand, many jurisdictions have chosen to allow paid testimonials if the law firm discloses that it is a paid testimonial. At the end of the day, you will have to determine what your jurisdiction allows.

An additional important caveat that may help you breathe a sigh of relief is that, under the Model Rules, you are permitted to provide nominal gifts to express appreciation. This particular provision has been adopted by a few jurisdictions so there is hope. If you are allowed to in your jurisdiction, keep this in mind: these items should be unanticipated and not be provided in exchange for something. How would this impact your video creation? Let's say you want to give people a $20 gift card for making a video for you. Model Rule 7.2(b)(5) states that the gift should not be "intended or reasonably expected to be a form of compensation for recommending a lawyer's services." Best practices complying with these model rules would mean you would not use the $20 gift card as an incentive up front for creating a video. Don't promise clients a gift for creating a testimonial video or sending someone your way. However, if they do a testimonial video describing how awesome it is working with you, feel free to say thank you with a simple gift of nominal value.

At the end of the day, it serves public policy to inform people about where and how they can access reliable legal services. The goal is not to stop people from knowing about you; it's to ensure that the communication is as pure as possible. Even when we look beyond the legal world, other industries have the same goal of making these transactions as straightforward as possible. The Federal Trade Commission (FTC) even requires that you must make disclaimers if a gift or some form of consideration is exchanged for a recommendation.[47] In our case, we aren't allowed to get too close to that line.

Are You an Expert?

It is essential to analyze how you hold yourself to the world. Model Rule 7.2(c) says, "A lawyer shall not state or imply that a lawyer is certified as a specialist in a particular field" unless they fall within a few narrow exceptions.[48] The rule limits

[47] "FTC's Endorsement Guides: What People Are Asking," Federal Trade Commission, June 2023, https://www.ftc.gov/business-guidance/resources/ftcs-endorsement-guides-what-people-are-asking.

[48] "Comment on Rule 7.2: Communications Concerning a Lawyer's Services: Specific Rules," American Bar Association, https://www.americanbar.org/groups/professional_responsibility/publications/model_rules_of_professional_conduct/rule_7_2_advertising/comment_on_rule_7_2/.

how attorneys present themselves unless they are certified as a specialist by a state or an organization accredited by the ABA. The comments further state:

> A lawyer is generally permitted to state that the lawyer "concentrates in" or is a "specialist," practices a "specialty," or "specializes in: particular fields based on the lawyer's experience, specialized training or education, but such communications are subject to the "false and misleading" standard applied in Rule 7.1 to communications concerning a lawyer's services.[49]

In other words, do not create videos that say you are an expert unless you understand the specific rules in your jurisdiction and qualify to do so. Some jurisdictions allow attorneys who are board certified to make those claims; some don't. As a legal professional, be precise, state what practice areas you work in, and if you have valuable credentials, state precisely what those credentials are, who provides them, and what they mean about the way you practice. If you are unsure, do not use terms like "expert," "expertise," and "specialist" that leave things open to broad interpretation and could lead reasonable viewers of your content to misunderstand your ability to handle their case. This rule also applies in some cases to what your clients say. Your clients cannot record testimonial or endorsement videos where they say that you are an expert.[50]

ABA MODEL RULE 7.3: SOLICITATION OF CLIENTS

Remember additional ethical rules about solicitation when deciding how to place and use videos. As attorneys, we are required to refrain from solicitation. Model Rule 7.3 states that:

> (a) "Solicitation" or "solicit" denotes a communication initiated by or on behalf of a lawyer or law firm that is directed to a specific person the lawyer knows or reasonably should know needs legal services in a

[49] Ibid.

[50] "Rule 7.2: Communications Concerning a Lawyer's Services: Specific Rules," American Bar Association, https://www.americanbar.org/groups/professional_responsibility/publications/model_rules_of_professional_conduct/rule_7_2_advertising/.

particular matter and that offers to provide, or reasonably can be understood as offering to provide, legal services for that matter.
(b) A lawyer shall not solicit professional employment by live person-to-person contact when a significant motive for the lawyer's doing so is the lawyer's or law firm's pecuniary gain, unless the contact is with a:
 (1) lawyer;
 (2) person who has a family, close personal, or prior business or professional relationship with the lawyer or law firm; or
 (3) person who routinely uses for business purposes the type of legal services offered by the lawyer.
(c) A lawyer shall not solicit professional employment even when not otherwise prohibited by paragraph (b), if:
 (1) the target of the solicitation has made known to the lawyer a desire not to be solicited by the lawyer; or
 (2) the solicitation involves coercion, duress or harassment.
(d) This Rule does not prohibit communications authorized by law or ordered by a court or other tribunal.
(e) Notwithstanding the prohibitions in this Rule, a lawyer may participate with a prepaid or group legal service plan operated by an organization not owned or directed by the lawyer that uses live person-to-person contact to enroll members or sell subscriptions for the plan from persons who are not known to need legal services in a particular matter covered by the plan.[51]

What does it mean to solicit? The model rules say that solicitation is communication from a law firm that is "directed to a specific person the lawyer knows or reasonably should know needs legal services." This book discusses creating personalized videos to create and deepen relationships, but can you use these videos to solicit people? The dreaded legal answer is very apt here. The model rules specifically prohibit **"live, person-to-person solicitation,"** so a nonlive video emailed could technically be an acceptable form of solicitation. There is no bright line rule, but there are a few things to consider in your analysis, particularly with personalized videos.

Legal Ethics Attorney Michael Downey explains it this way:

The key should be why the email is being sent to the person. If you know they need legal representation in a particular matter and are

[51] "Rule 7.3: Solicitation of Clients," American Bar Association, www.americanbar.org/groups/professional_responsibility/publications/model_rules_of_professional_conduct/rule_7_3_direct_contact_with_prospective_clients/.

sending the personalized video to seek employment in that matter, it would likely be a (non-real-time) solicitation governed by Rule 7.3(b). However, if you are simply sending a video to someone who may generally need the type of legal services—for example, sending a video to a corporate officer because you suspect they need contracts reviewed or employment law matters addressed, this would be a Rule 7.2 communication and probably allowed.

The ultimate determining factor would be what language your specific jurisdiction has applied, the specific context around the content and your intended recipient, and any relevant opinions regarding solicitation. The model rules have a few exceptions for people like family and real friends or people who regularly use your legal services. The model rules also add that if someone says they do not want to hear from you, or your communication "involves coercion, duress, or harassment," do not do it.

If you have an email list, you may wonder whether you can send videos to that audience. Or perhaps you are building a YouTube community. The comments state that "person-to-person contact does not include chat rooms, text messages or other written communications that recipients may easily disregard."These rules do not apply if someone has requested information from you. Therefore, in the cases in which someone has subscribed to your email list to receive ongoing information from you, you may communicate offers that fall within the scope of permission they have granted.

There are other provisions of these model rules, but these are most pertinent to you as you create video content to market yourself and your legal services. Remember, we have been looking at this from the perspective of the model rules—which are not binding. However, most states have adopted these rules or a portion of these rules in their local regulations. To see where the jurisdictions you practice in falls, check your local rules.

DISCLAIMERS IN MARKETING VIDEOS: ANOTHER LAYER OF PROTECTION

If you choose to use video in your marketing strategy, it would be extremely beneficial to become familiar with and implement disclaimers. Disclaimers used in legal marketing videos help you clearly communicate with prospective clients the limits of what you are offering during the marketing interactions. Certain ethics rules also require the use of disclaimers.

As noted earlier, there is a wide range of ethical considerations that are still applicable to attorneys even if they are using video, so be as clear and consistent as possible in your use of disclaimers. In video creation and legal marketing, disclaimers are your friend. Use them often. Here are a few instances when you may apply disclaimers to your videos.

Disclaimers Regarding the Attorney–Client Relationship

If you are providing information to prospective clients regardless of whether the content would constitute attorney advertising, you should include a disclaimer that explicitly states that no attorney–client relationship is formed through the content provided. You can choose to clearly say this audibly in the video, or have this language appear in the video or in the description or caption associated with the video.

Along these same lines, consider also using disclaimer language to clearly articulate the purpose of the video that you are sharing. Standard disclaimers may provide that the information provided is for educational purposes. Another typical disclaimer involves ensuring potential clients know that speaking to you via video does not create an attorney–client relationship.

The disclaimer language I have used states something along the following lines: "Please note the information I provide on this video is for educational purposes only. It does not create an attorney–client relationship. Everyone's situation is different and requires an individualized analysis. Contact a licensed attorney in your jurisdiction if you are facing a legal issue."[52]

Disclaimers for Using Client Testimonials

Client video testimonials and videos that provide endorsements or insights as to what representation from your firm looks like also require significant disclaimers. Jurisdictions may vary as to specific language required, but there are many points of agreement. For one, all jurisdictions seem to agree that content regarding results or outcomes should come with language that helps your prospective clients know

[52] The Law Office of Temi Siyanbade. "YouTube Disclaimer." The Law Office of Temi Siyanbade, *YouTube*, Upload Date (June-21-23), www.youtube.com/watch?v=-Qpvm743Uco&ab_channel=TheLawOfficeofTemiSiyanbade.

that results may vary. Language that also states that there are no guarantees can also be employed.

ADDITIONAL ETHICAL CONSIDERATIONS

As you create your videos, here are a few other things to remember. You may find that some of these things are specifically called out in your local jurisdiction.

The Reasonable Person

Generally speaking, when analyzing how this will be perceived, most jurisdictions will interpret your communications from the perspective of the reasonable person. This means that, as we have established throughout this book, put yourself in your potential client's shoes. If the marketing can be perceived to lead them to false conclusions, your jurisdiction will probably interpret it as you, so be very careful.

Subject to Local Jurisdiction

Check this information against your local jurisdiction rules. Some states have fewer restrictions that empower you to connect with potential clients. Do not miss those opportunities. Others may find that their states have more narrow and stringent rules. Do not fall into the traps. Be proactive. Many states have confidential phone lines where you can ask your questions about what is permissible.

Ongoing Support

When it comes to these ethical requirements, the work is never perfectly done. We have ongoing requirements to stay on top of developments in these areas. To continue to access information, do not hesitate to stay connected with your local colleagues. The ABA's Law Practice Management Division has a Legal Technology Resource Center (LTRC). If you can, participate in conferences such as the ABA annual TECHSHOW. Environments like these create opportunities for attorneys to stay on top of developments in the video arena for attorneys.

Although the information in this chapter may seem dense and you still must check and comply with your local rules, remember that it is a good thing for clients to learn about what services you provide, and your use of videos is furthering that good, professional goal. By having this rules survey, you'll have methods most aligned with clarity for you and your clients.

3

The Essential Tools

When you start creating video content, it is easy to become overwhelmed by the sheer number of options available when selecting the right tools. For someone just starting, it is critical to avoid purchasing overly complicated gadgets. Instead, start with the basics; as you gain experience and more confidence, you can upgrade your tools.

Whether you're using video for communications, marketing, or both, there are a few essential elements to address. You will need

- Your camera
- Your lighting
- Your sound
- Your tripod

YOUR BASIC VIDEO SETUP

This is one of the most important sections of the book, and with the tips here, anyone, and I mean anyone, will be able to create excellent videos without having to break the bank. I say this because this is where I started. As I described earlier, I am not a photographer or videographer by trade or training. I'm an educator-turned-attorney who needed to be creative and had an interest in technology. This section will explore the tools and tech I have used (and some I have not) to make your videos reflect the quality and professionalism you desire.

This introductory video setup is suitable for video conferencing and for marketing videos that use the "talking head" format where a person (probably you) speaks directly into the camera.

Your Camera

There's no better place to start when talking about the essentials of making videos than starting with the camera. Many people think they need a super fancy camera with all the bells and whistles, but that is not the case. If you understand a few basic concepts about the other elements of video, you will find that you can create high-quality videos without complex tools (or high cost). Even for marketing your firm with video, you can use the cameras you have to create high-quality videos that help you connect with your audience.

Because here's the thing: your audience might not even be equipped to watch a video made with the fanciest gadgets. Right now, the most popular high-end cameras produce film in 4K resolution, meaning that the image produced has a significant number of pixels to create super sharp images. However, most video content is consumed on the go on someone's phone. The 4K details you'll spend an arm and a leg for are barely visible to your audience on such small screens, so do not stress over these details when you start.

I want to reiterate that point because I have spoken with legal professionals who are scared that their videos won't portray the level of professionalism they desire. To that fear, I have two responses. First, most consumers are more concerned with the factors we will introduce in Chapter 9: the elements of know, like, and trust. If you focus on connecting on those levels, you alleviate the pressure to manufacture inauthentic personas. Second, you can still create excellent videos with a great web camera or phone camera.

Speaking of web cameras or cameras on your phone, if you are starting your video-making journey, start there. Most computers manufactured today have a built-in web camera embedded in the monitor. Regardless of the manufacturer, your standard laptop will also have a web camera built in. Those can be sufficient to get you started. This is often your most basic camera and will get the job done. However, you can add a few tools to your toolbox to enhance the quality of your overall output.

Before you hit "Record," make sure your camera lens is clean. This tip may seem basic, but sometimes our images are blurry and poor because a forgotten fingerprint is trying to leave its mark on your video. Start by finding a soft cloth and wiping your lens.

One thing you can add to improve your primary web camera output is a detachable lens. In your selection, look for telephoto lenses. These lenses can make the frame of reference for your video more comprehensive, which in some cases can make them appear more sophisticated. Many of these lenses can also be used on your cellphone and can be purchased for about $20. Using these lenses is also extremely simple. These lenses are screwed or clipped on to your phone, and voila—your camera frame is more expansive.

The next tool I will share was a total game changer for me in upgrading the camera. You can purchase web cameras that can significantly improve video quality for a few extra dollars. A familiar favorite brand is Logitech. The Logitech C920 and C922 are consistently referred to as top budget-friendly options. Another excellent option is the Logitech Brio. These cameras are simple to use and often have plug and play features. What does that mean? Using these cameras is often as simple as plugging the camera into your computer. Once you do that, most modern systems automatically read the video source and switch cameras from the built-in one to the one you have now plugged in. Occasionally, you have to switch the cameras manually, but many of your recording systems have that information easily accessible.

Finally, think about how great your video input would look if you could use your cellphone as a web camera. With today's technological advancements, the cameras on our phones have impressive capabilities. You can use them to create crisp, high-quality video recordings that, if done right, may be indistinguishable from your more complex cameras.

A few apps have made it relatively simple to convert your phone's camera into a web camera so that you do not have to spend a dime on improving the quality of your video. The first app is called Camo. It was recently made available to both Apple and Android users. Download this app and connect your phone to your laptop. After walking through the simple step-by-step installation, be prepared to be amazed. If you have a newer cellphone, it will not be a fair fight. Your phone will exceed your expectations by far. A similar app that offers a wireless connection is EpocCam and EpocCam Pro. The only downside is that there may be a slight lag associated with these tools because they were not originally designed to be web cameras.

It's important to note that if you are recording using a tool that does not plug into your computer, you will need to transfer your video. This may sound overwhelming at first, but it doesn't need to be. There are a few different ways to approach this. In this section, we will focus on transferring from your standard camera phone, but we will address more complex transfer later in this chapter when we discuss leveling up your production.

When transferring files from your camera phone, your phone may make this a bit easy for you with automatic cloud storage. This means that your phone may already be set to upload whatever you capture onto a platform like iCloud or Google Photos. If this is the case, you can log on to your Google account, or open Photos on your Apple device. Ensure that your devices are up to date. Then check your device and gallery settings on your phones to ensure that they are set to back your photos up to the right platform.

Your phones will likely also provide several ways to share files by default. To discover the various methods you can use to share your files, find the video file you would like to transfer and hit the "Share" button. Most phones will provide different apps to select from. If you have an application like Dropbox on your phone, you can choose to share the file to that location. You may also find that the video you have recorded is ready for general publication to a social app you already have on your phone. In this case, share your content directly. These are the most direct ways to move a file from your phone, but this is not by any means an exclusive list. As you grow in your video creation journey, you may discover a few more options that better suit you.

To learn more about the tools mentioned earlier and to explore additional options, check out the following resources for in-depth reviews and guidance:

- TechRadar[1]
- *PCMag*[2]
- CNET[3]

Your Lighting

After selecting the right camera for your basic setup, it is time to consider lighting. Mastering your lighting setup can significantly enhance your video and level up the perception of your video. Much of the graininess you may currently be observing stems from the lack of proper positioning or insufficient light.

In addressing lighting in your video, it's important to acknowledge that different skin tones require different lighting. Lighting setups that work for individuals with lighter skin tones may not always work the same for individuals with darker

---

[1] Christian Guyton, "What Webcam? 5 Reviewed and Rated," "The Best Webcams 2024: Top Video Cameras for PCs," *TechRadar*, updated May 22, 2024, www.techradar.com/news/computing-components/peripherals/what-webcam-5-reviewed-and-rated-1027972/.

[2] Will Greenwald, "The Best Webcams for 2024," *PCMag*, updated July 10, 2024, www.pcmag.com/picks/the-best-webcams/.

[3] James Bricknell and Justin Jaffe, "Best Gear for Online Classes or Meetings in 2024," *CNET*, April 12, 2024, www.cnet.com/tech/computing/best-webcam-and-gear-for-online-meetings/.

skin tones, and that is okay.[4] The key is finding a lighting setup that portrays you in the most authentic and flattering way. As you test different setups, pay attention to whether the lighting washes you out, makes you look bland, or distorts the way you really look.

One of the quickest lighting improvements for your videos is to make sure the light is coming from the right place. Let's imagine that you only have the main overhead light and natural light coming from a window or windows on one side of the room. Believe it or not, this is enough to get great visuals.

Natural light can be a fantastic low-budget tool if you have access to a space that allows you to capitalize on lighting flowing through a window. Make sure that if you are using natural light as your primary light source, that light should be in front of you and behind your camera. This means that you should be able to look out the window—not share the beautiful view with your audience. This principle regarding light placement is essential. Even if you decide to add additional lights to your setup, your main subject should generally be in front of the main light source.

Now even though I am a natural light fan and I believe it is impressive as a tool, it is not without problems. Some in the content creation world are not huge fans of natural light because you cannot control natural light. For example, you may have plans to record, but a perfectly sunny day can quickly become wet and dark. In such instances, having an alternative basic setup can be a lifesaver.

As an alternative, consider using your desk lamp as a source of additional light in an introductory video setup. The simple inclusion of a desk lamp can make a huge difference in the quality of your video. At the peak of the COVID-19 pandemic, this was my standard practice when I spent more time working from home. My home desk was not conducive to my typical setup and did not have room for bulky lighting equipment. However, I had my standard desk light, which I was able to position behind my camera. This instantly enhanced the quality of my live stream video conferences.

If you choose to use a desk lamp as an additional light source, change the lightbulbs in the room and in the desk lamp to daylight lightbulbs. These bulbs were designed to act like natural light and can significantly improve your appearance without being subject to vagaries of the weather. This setup is usually sufficient for effective video conferencing and simple videos.

---

[4] Community Voice, "Zoom Lighting Tips, Especially for People of Color," *The Voice*, December 21, 2020, www.communityvoiceks.com/2020/12/21/zoom-lighting-tips-especially-for-people-of-color/.

You may also explore using LED lights, and there are several to choose from. The two most common types are ring lights and panel lights.[5] Ring lights, as their name suggests, are LED lights shaped like rings and are often cheaper and more accessible to maneuver than other lights. Ring lights were made famous by YouTubers and social media influencers—especially in the beauty industry, because of the way the lights made their subjects appear. Many of these lights have accessories that allow you to position your camera in the middle of the light. The ring shape of the light encircles the subject being recorded and allows you to create a flattering, soft, airy light around the edge of your face. The positioning rules still apply if you choose to use a ring light. It is best if you face the ring light.

Another unique attribute of using ring lights is how they are often reflected in the eyes of the user. In other words, if you look closely into the eyes of the person in front of the ring light, you will see the lights. Note that the appearance of a ring light in your eyes during a video may be distracting. However, its significance depends on the context and the specific audience you have in mind. It is generally advisable that you minimize any distractions including the reflection of a ring light in your eyes.

If you wear glasses, you may develop a love–hate relationship with ring lights because they can create an intense glare on Zoom. However, you can improve the way your glasses appear on the video conferences. One way to do that is by changing your lights. Instead of using one ring light, switch your ring lights to LED panel lights.

A panel light has the same LED technology so it can also provide sufficient lighting but may not have the same framing. These lights improve the light's quality by diffusing the light's intensity. As a result, the intensity that creates the glare is reduced. Often, these lights do not get as hot as other lights, making them easier to manage. Generally, panel lights may be more appropriate if you plan to use them for videos that capture your full body. However, for a simple video conferencing setup or a basic talking head video, a portable plug-in or clip-on light may be sufficient.

Your Sound

Your sound quality impacts how your audience receives your video. If your sound is solid and clear and accompanies a reliable camera, people will be inclined to listen to what you share. The first thing you can do to manage the quality of your

[5] "Why Are Ring Lights So Popular?," *Vloggermail*, newsletter, Techwire, https://vloggermail.com/why-are-ring-lights-so-popular/.

sound is to improve your environment. Make sure you are in a quiet place with limited distractions.

Next, it is essential to incorporate some form of an external microphone. Your old, wired microphones produce excellent sound. A wired microphone is a microphone with a cord that is plug directly into your recording device. That recording device could be your cellphone, computer, or camera.

You may also be considering using wired earphones with a built-in microphone, a blue-tooth earbud, or headphone that has a built-in microphone, or a standard headset with microphone attached.

However, in my experience, the quality of these two-in-one tools often varies and does not always produce the best sounds. Although they seem like the best of both worlds (the ability to hear and a built-in microphone), they often produce poor-sounding audio. My recommendation is to test your tools by recording yourself speaking in a video conferencing room. After I listened to playbacks, I decided to personally limit the use of such microphones to low-pressure video conferences.

To improve the sound quality of your recording, as we discussed above, consider using a USB microphone. These devices allow you to record directly into your computer. How these microphones pick up sound varies. Look for microphones with a cardioid polar pattern, meaning that the microphone is designed to pick up sound coming from directly in front of it and diminish the sounds coming from behind it. By having this feature built in, your microphone, when positioned correctly, will focus on the sounds coming directly to it and reduce the ambient noise of the environment.

Any cardioid microphone should satisfy your needs. The popular Blue Yeti and Blue Snowball USB microphones include the cardioid pattern and the ability to convert to other patterns as well.[6] The various polar pattern settings are beneficial if you plan on using this microphone for more dynamic videos such as podcast interviews in a shared space. Two additional alternatives are the Shure MV7 USB microphone[7] and the RØDE PodMic Cardioid Dynamic Broadcast Microphone.[8] These two mics produce excellent sound and are simple plug and play USB microphones like the Blue Yeti.

---

[6] Logitech C920S HD Pro Webcam with Privacy Shutter—Widescreen Video Calling and Recording, 1080p Streaming Camera, Desktop or Laptop Webcam.

[7] Shure MV7 USB Microphone for Podcasting, Recording, Live Streaming & Gaming, Built-in Headphone Output, All Metal USB/XLR Dynamic Mic, Voice-Isolating Technology, TeamSpeak & Zoom Certified—Black.

[8] PodMic, RØDE, https://rode.com/en-us/microphones/broadcast/podmic.

When adding an external microphone, pay attention to microphone placement. You do not want your microphone too close or too far away when using these USB microphones. If your microphone is too close, you will notice that certain consonant sounds sound more forceful and harsher. If you are too far away, the microphone will not be able to pick up your sound. Try to have your microphone at least 2 inches but no more than 10 inches away from your mouth. This placement will help improve how the microphone picks up the background noise.

Your Tripod

Finally, let us discuss what type of tripod you should use to start off. Whether you need a tripod and, if so, the type of tripod you use is dependent on the type of video you are recording. If you are recording a video on the go, you may find that a tripod is not a top priority. For example, I know a few attorneys who simply share insights about legal news or frequently asked questions via social media. These attorneys do not need tripods. However, if you are using video for more continuous video conferences or talking head videos, there are a few different simple options to consider.

If your setup involves using a USB webcam and plugging it into your computer, you could elevate your camera by elevating your laptop. A common starter setup is using a stack of books under your laptop. In fact, this was my first video setup when I became serious about creating videos as a legal professional. It was more than enough to get the job done because I would place a box or a stack of books on a table. I then placed my laptop on top.

An alternative to that setup is to invest in a laptop stand. By purchasing a laptop stand, you can have a more permanent solution (and enjoy the added benefit of reducing the strain you are having on your body and creating space for your laptop to ventilate).[9] You can find laptop stands as inexpensive as $12.[10] Some of these stands are also extremely lightweight and portable, making it easy to create an excellent video setup anywhere.

Finally, for a simple setup, you may choose to invest in a simple tripod purchased online. Many online tripods come with adapters to help you mount your cell phone. There are also small tripods for use on a desk or table. This option maybe most feasible for individuals using desktop computers and larger monitors where setting up your camera over your monitor is not feasible. In these instances,

---

[9] Hashir Ibrahim, "7 Pros and Cons of Using a Laptop Stand," *MakeUseOf*, September 20, 2022, https://www.makeuseof.com/pros-cons-of-laptop-stand/.

[10] Laptop Stand for Desk, Adjustable Laptop Stand for Desk, Laptop Riser for MacBook Pro and Air 13 15 17 inch, Laptop Stands Adjustable, Ergonomic Computer Stand, Notebook Stand Patented SecureStop.

a separate tripod is a valid option because your web cameras typically come with a tripod mount.

Most, if not all, of your cameras and web cameras will come ready for tripod mounting. You will also notice that you can find tripods of all shapes and sizes. When shopping for a tripod, consider how much you want to spend, whether the tripod will be on the desk or on the floor, how tall you need the tripod to be, and the weight and size of the camera to be used. For larger cameras or cell phones, you may choose to invest in larger, more sturdy tripods.

If you are concerned about desk space, there are effective tripod solutions that take up minimal room. For example, the JOBY GorillaPod offers flexible, wrapping legs that can cling to objects as an alternative to a traditional rigid tripod. It collapses down to just 11.7 inches but can hold cameras up to 6.6 pounds.

Another great space-saving option is the K&F Concept DSLR Tripod Mini, which folds down small enough to fit in a bag at 15.35 inches but extends up to 50 inches high while holding over 17 pounds. So, with some research, you can find tripods sturdy enough for a quality webcam setup that only take up a tiny footprint on your desk.

LEVELING UP YOUR VIDEO PRODUCTION

We have addressed a straightforward but highly effective video setup; however, you may be interested in how to produce videos with slightly more edge or refinement. This section focuses on those elements. As we walk through the concepts here, recognize that these are enhancements, not requirements.

Many seasoned content creators will emphasize that their success is based more significantly on the substance of the content they created rather than the form. I emphasize this point: Do not hold off on your video production because you want to have a "leveled up" production system. Start where you are and build toward it. Add the following items in increments, if possible, to master each addition tastefully. Also note that tools cannot be separated from technique. In other words, getting a better tool but not knowing how to use it does not benefit you.

Enhanced Lighting

To enhance your video, the first thing to do is to improve your lighting. Lighting makes a significant difference in how your video looks, but it is often overlooked. Slight modifications or investments in this area can significantly enhance the output of your video. In this section, let's address some of the most important lighting upgrades that make the most significant differences in your video.

One thing you can do is adjust the position of your lights. After you introduce LED lights to your setup, you may notice a certain intensity or harshness in the visuals. Even though you can see things more clearly, you may have noticed excessive shadows around your face. This effect is referred to as hard or harsh light. Tyler Herrinton, a popular YouTuber, explains the phenomenon this way: "When we are describing hard light and soft light, what we are really describing is the quality of the shadows produced by a light source."[11]

In seeking to be intentional as a communicator, ask yourself whether these shadows support the message, story, or theme of your video. Moving the positioning of your primary light impacts this. If your light is currently pointed directly at you, consider positioning it slightly above eye level at a 45-degree angle so that it is now slightly pointing down on you. This slight adjustment will help you impact the intensity of the light on your subject.

Another way to reduce the harshness of a light is to spread the light source out over a wider area. In other words, make the light seem bigger. One way to do that is to use a light that does some of the work for you. The Lume Cube Edge Light is a popular option for those interested in a quick and easy setup.[12] These lights mount to your desk and can double as a desk light and light for video conferences. Additionally, it illuminates you as the subject of your video without the same harsh shadows forming. If you can, consider purchasing another light to further enhance the way you look. By positioning two lights with reduced intensity pointed toward you or your subject, the lights from the two sources diffuse the personal impact of the lights. If set appropriately, the lights will cancel out the effect of glare on your images. This is especially true when two Lume Cube Edge Lights are positioned to reduce glare and spread the light.

Alternatively, for those inclined to create DIY lights, you can go to your local hardware store to create your own set of soft lighting source. When I began to produce videos consistently, I knew that I needed better lighting to improve the quality of my videos. If you have more time than funds, a DIY tutorial like the one created by video marketing company Wistia may be extremely helpful in creating makeshift soft box lights.[13]

---

[11] Tyler Herrinton, "The Secret to Soft Lightening for Video Calls & YouTube Videos," YouTube video, 13:22, uploaded December 7, 2020, www.youtube.com/watch?v=X1OCC5UN0to&ab_channel=TylerHerrinton.

[12] "Lume Cube 12" Mini Portable Edge-Lit-Bi-Color LED Ring Light with Stand," *Adoroma*, https://www.adorama.com/lcringmini.html.

[13] Chris Lavigne, "The Down and Dirty DIY Lighting Kit," *Wistia*, May 26, 2022, www.wistia.com/learn/production/down-and-dirty-lighting-kit/.

You can also adjust the color temperature. Recall the earlier discussion of daylight lightbulbs. Well, the difference between that daylight lightbulb and standard bulbs is color temperature. You can find lighting sources that allow you to control the temperature, thereby making it easier for you to control the overall visual output. Adjusting color temperature may also help if your initial setup did not create the most authentic and flattering reflection of your skin tone.[14] As a woman of color, I have found that color temperature adjustments really help me create the best lighting setups for me. I often find that putting my light settings to more cool tones can be beneficial, but this also depends upon the natural light available in your environment.

Let's discuss a few more positioning concepts. There are three main types of lighting positions to consider. Mastering this three-point lighting setup may be one of the more cost-effective ways of enhancing the quality of your video without changing your other essential tools. These three key lighting points are your key light, fill light, and backlight. Your key light is the light that is focused primarily on your subject. Your backlight is light positioned behind your subject, which helps create depth around your topic and increase separation between your subject and the background. Finally, your fill light provides additional light to set the mood and potentially help finer details in your environment stand out. This fill light is often positioned in a way that allows it to balance out the shadows created by your leading key light. The positioning of these three videos is called three-point lighting.

The graphic on the following page identifies how you should arrange your three-point lighting.

Next, what type of lights should there be? If we are moving beyond our ring lights, you have a few different options. The easiest way to tackle this is to purchase a prepackaged three-point lighting set. There is a wide range of options available online.

A few other considerations are ways to construct your three-point lighting system. You can move these lights closer or farther from your subject to determine the intensity desired. As alluded to earlier, some of the LED panel kits you purchase will come with digital controls that help you adjust the warmth of the light provided so that the colors are recorded to reflect the natural color of your environment or the mood you want to set.

---

[14] Community Voice, "Zoom Lighting Tips, Especially for People of Color," *The Voice*, December 21, 2020, www.communityvoiceks.com/2020/12/21/zoom-lighting-tips-especially-for-people-of-color/.

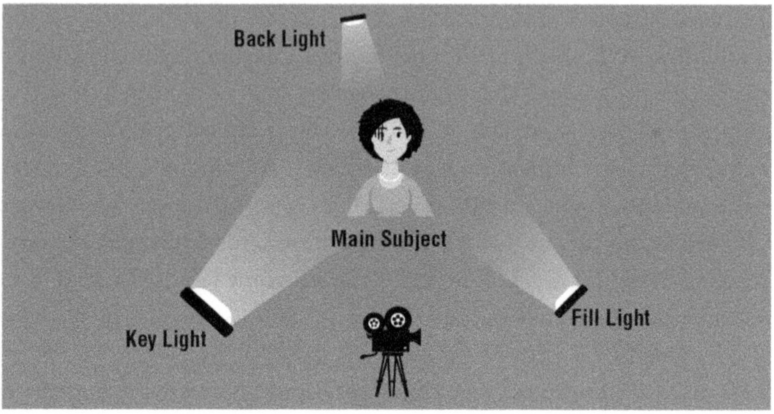

When looking for a light setup consider the following factors:

- Size
- Cost
- Versatility
- Options to adjust color temperature

Please note that these lights will take up more space than ring lights, so consider compatibility with your overall recording setup. Don't forget to read through reviews and product descriptions to choose the one that best suits your needs. You can find a variety of valuable options on Amazon.com.[15]

Enhanced Sound

Taking your sound to the next level will involve investing in both your tools and your skillset. In this section, we will focus on the tools. Let's start by discussing different types of microphones you may consider investing in to enhance the sound captured by your recording device.

The first option we will explore is the Lavalier (lapel) microphones. A Lavalier microphone is a microphone that is placed on the subject. These microphones can be excellent if you create dynamic videos and want more freedom to move around. You can find wired Lavalier microphones or wireless Lavaliers. If you are using a wired Lavalier microphone, the microphone is clipped to the speaker's

[15] Andoer Softbox Photography Lighting Kit Professional Studio Equipment with 20″ × 28″ Softbox, 2800-5700K 85W Bi-Color Temperature Bulb with Remote, Light Stand, Boom Arm for Portrait Product Shooting.

clothing, usually on their chest.[16] It should ideally be a handspan distance between the speaker's mouth and the Lavalier mic.

With Lavalier microphones, pay attention to elements that may distort the sound or the visual. When it comes to the sound, make sure there are no other pieces of clothing rubbing up against the microphone in use. The movement may muffle the sound and create inconsistencies in the recording. Make sure the cord from the wired Lavalier mic is controlled and concealed. You may do this by lining the cord along the inside of jacket, behind a tie, or underneath the speaker's shirt. Tape may be used to keep the microphone in place.[17]

The next thing to consider with your Lavalier microphone is what you are recording into. The cable you use to connect the source will depend on whether you are recording into your phone, laptop, or camera. Depending on your distance from the recording source, you may find that you need an extension cord for your microphone. An alternative to finding a way to extend the cord is using a wireless option that requires a transmitter.[18] Although the quality of both wired and wireless Lavalier microphones has improved, some believe the wireless options are more susceptible to more diminished quality.

The second microphone to discuss is the shotgun microphone, which is a microphone designed to pick up sounds coming from a distance. They are often the microphones you see attached to the top of a camera. The distance these microphones are from the subject depends on the type of shotgun microphone in use.

These microphones are designed to capture the sound of items and objects directly in front of them. If you are creating more personal videos to bring your potential clients into the behind-the-scenes of your practice, you may find that using a shotgun microphone with one of the cameras discussed below is helpful. These two microphone types also vary in terms of quality and price point.

Enhanced Cameras

Often, when one is considering leveling up their video, an enhanced camera is the first element they want to jump to. However, investing in more advanced camera gear requires accompanying tools and has a learning curve. The most

[16] RØDE, "How to Use the RØDE Wireless GO II to Capture Great Audio | Beginner's Guide," YouTube video, 21:35, uploaded February 16, 2023, https://www.youtube.com/watch?v=wW3JZCSfHZs.

[17] RØDE, "How to Use a Lavalier Mic | How-To Guide," YouTube video, 5:31, uploaded May 15, 2019, www.youtube.com/watch?v=wd_f7iYbFrA&ab_channel=R%C3%98DE.

[18] Ibid.

common cameras to explore if you want to move beyond the web camera or cellphone are your vlogging (also called action cameras), DSLR, or mirrorless cameras.

The most cost-effective and easy camera is the vlogging camera. The most popular vlogging camera types are GoPro cameras. These cameras do not require additional equipment and are often small and extremely portable. The range of options available for customizing settings is limited. However, you can still record high-quality sharp images. This camera doesn't have the best sound, but you can use an external microphone with it. An action camera alternative is the Insta360.

The next two options, mirrorless cameras and DSLR cameras, have increased functionality but are usually more expensive and bulkier when it comes to handling. If you purchase one of these cameras, you must also buy accompanying items to incorporate them into your system. Be prepared to invest in

- The appropriate camera lenses
- The right capture cards to connect your camera to your computer so that your computer can read the data from your camera (that is, if you are interested in using your camera to live stream)
- Ongoing power sources to keep your camera on when you are recording
- Memory cards to store and transfer the videos

One thing I hope this highlights is that these cameras are not web cameras. They are not plug and play. The items I mentioned above will also vary depending on your camera type. For example, you cannot just purchase one camera and get another lens without confirming that it is indeed compatible with your camera. Similarly, not every capture card is compatible with every system. You cannot assume that everything works together.

Without the proper lens, the framing and your image's appearance may not match what you are looking for. One way you might see this, for example, is that you may be seeking a video that looks wide and has that nice blurry background effect you have seen in some YouTube videos. Well, to produce that effect, it is not enough to have a nice camera—you have to select the right wide-angle lens that opens up the shot.

Here are my tips and considerations if you are wading into this realm:

- Purchase a camera that is more beginner friendly. A few beginner favorites include the Canon M50 series (my current camera choice) or the Sony ZV-E10.

- If possible, find cameras that have side articulating flip screens. This means you can open the screen and pull it to the side or up to see what you are recording. The benefit of this feature is that you will not have to purchase an additional portable monitor to know what you are recording.
- Canon recently enabled its mirrorless and DSLR cameras to be able to be captured using a USB plug. You may have to search for a compatible USB cable, but that is easier than navigating the world of capture cards.

Additionally, in this world of more complex cameras, there are a few terms you will have to master and understand to maximize your higher end camera production capabilities. The first one is "resolution." Resolution is all about the detail your videos are able to pick up. The experts at Descript define resolution as "the total number of pixels in a video frame rate": the higher the number, the greater the detail your camera is able to pick up.[19] Most people are viewing videos from devices that are not able to show beyond 1080p, but that number is quickly changing. When reviewing cameras, explore the resolution they are able to produce. However, please keep in mind that higher video resolutions require more computer memory during the editing and processing stages.

Next, consider the term "white balance." White balance involves ensuring the colors taken in accurately reflect what you see or the mood you are developing. The white balance is one of the first things you will want to adjust or set in your camera.

The next term to familiarize yourself with is "frame rate" or "frames per second." A camera's frame rate is "the measurement of how quickly a number of frames appears within a second, which is why it's also called FPS (frames per second)."[20] When recording using more advanced tools, be sure that your rate is set to 30 fps or more. However, know that adjusting the frame rate creates opportunities for slow-motion videos or timelapse videos.

Finally, work toward understanding and adjusting items related to the lighting settings in your camera. Here's a quick glossary:

- **Exposure**: Exposure is "the level of brightness [or darkness] across a frame."[21] Your exposure determines whether a shot looks too light, too

[19] Vanessa Hojda, "Video Resolution 101: What It Is and How it Impacts Video Quality," *Descript* (blog), September 19, 2023, https://www.descript.com/blog/article/video-resolution.

[20] Margaret Kurniawan and Hiroshi Hara, "What Is Frame Rate?" *Adobe*, n.d., https://www.adobe.com/creativecloud/video/discover/frame-rate.html.

[21] Gray Kotzé, "How Cinematographers Set Their Exposure," *In Depth Cine*, https://www.indepthcine.com/videos/exposure.

dark, or just right. Exposure is impacted by several factors but the ones to truly master are its shutter speed, aperture, and ISO.

- **Shutter Speed**: Your shutter speed is a measure of how long your camera allows its sensor to be exposed to light. The faster your shutter closes, the less light it takes in and vice versa.[22] Adjusting your shutter speed can also impact how well motion is captured in your images. Faster shutter speeds eliminate the blur of motion, and slower speeds make motion more apparent.
- **Aperture:** A camera's aperture has been described as the "pupil of your lens" because of the way it works. It is the opening where light comes through to enter your camera, and it can be adjusted to allow more light or less light depending on your needs.[23] Adjusting your aperture can impact how bright your visuals appear and the depth of field. So, when you see images that show the focus in front clearly, but the background is really blurry, that is typically a function of a large aperture. When someone has a video that captures all the details of an intricate landscape, they usually have a small aperture. One thing to note, though, is that aperture numbers can be deceiving. Often described with an f/ before a number, the larger the number, the smaller the aperture. So an f/16 has a smaller aperture than an f/2.
- **ISO:** The last term you should start familiarizing yourself with is the International Organization for Standardization (ISO), which is your camera's sensitivity to light.[24] This will also impact the brightness or darkness of your video clips. Most cameras will have the ability to adjust this, but will also have their ideal or native ISO. As a beginner, stay with the camera's native ISO.

Most cameras have defaults and auto features that make it possible to overlook understanding each of these details, but if you want to level up your setup, you should consider manually adjusting these elements. Every camera manufacturer and camera model differ and there is no way we could possibly cover all the variations that exist. What that means for you is that you will have to embark on some independent learning. Two great books for understanding the general

[22] Nasim Mansurov, "Introduction to Shutter Speed in Photography," *Photographylife*, October 4, 2023, https://photographylife.com/what-is-shutter-speed-in-photography.

[23] Nasim Mansurov, "Understanding Aperture in Photography," *Photographylife*, October 4, 2023, https://photographylife.com/what-is-aperture-in-photography.

[24] Trevor Holmes, "What Is ISO for Video?" *Wistia*, January 9, 2023, https://wistia.com/learn/production/what-is-iso.

features of DSLR cameras or mirrorless cameras are *DSLR Photography for Beginners*[25] and *Learning Photography, Shooting in Manual Mode: Beginner Photography Theory for SLR or Mirrorless Cameras.*[26] Additionally, do not neglect your camera's owner's manual. Finally, two of my favorite video platforms are Think Media with Sean Cannell[27] and Diana Gladney, author of *The One Right Video: An Entrepreneur's Guide to Grow Your Community, Get More Qualified Leads, and Close More Sales Using YouTube.*[28]

Enhanced Tripods

As with the other tools described earlier, leveling up your tripod is not required for excellent videos. However, what you may find is that enhanced tripods and camera mounts may enable you to create more unique shots. To start, if you are on the go, consider tripods that allow you to hold your camera and your light together. One common configuration involves ring lights that also serve as phone tripods. These combination options allow you to conserve space and control the height of your tripod.

If you are investing in a DSLR or mirrorless camera, you may find that you need to invest in a more heavy-duty tripod to sustain the weight and size of your camera. However, keep in mind that heavy-duty does not necessarily mean large. For example, a popular and portable, heavy-duty tripod is the JOBY GorillaPod Tripod.[29] This tripod is only 15.2 inches high, but it is advertised as being able to hold an 11-pound camera.[30] Another feature of the GorillaPod, also found in other tripods, are the flexible legs. The flexible JOBY legs allow you to set up your camera from different angles. For example, you may find that you prefer hanging your camera or using the JOBY tripod as a selfie-stick on the go.

---

[25] Brian Black, *DSLR Photography for Beginners: Take 10 Times Better Pictures in 48 Hours or Less! Best Way to Learn Digital Photography, Master Your DSLR Camera & Improve Your Digital SLR Photography Skills* (eBookIt.com, 2020).

[26] David Edwards, *Learning Photography, Shooting in Manual Mode: Beginner Photography Theory for SLR or Mirrorless Cameras* (Kindle edition, 2020).

[27] Think Media, www.thinkmedia.video/.

[28] Diana Gladney and Ray Edwards, *The One Right Video: An Entrepreneur's Guide to Grow Your Community, Get More Qualified Leads, and Close More Sales Using YouTube* (Video Simplified Publishing, 2023).

[29] "GorillaPod®," JOBY, www.joby.com/us-en/gorillapod/.

[30] "GorillaPod® 5K Kit," JOBY, https://joby.com/us-en/gorillapod-5k-kit-made-in-italy-jb91508-bww/.

Finally, consider purchasing a tripod that allows you to extend the height or shoot from unique angles. My favorite tripods in this category typically have a height range from 23 inches to 77 inches.[31] If you are creating more artistically complex videos, you may find yourself filming low to the ground to shoot unique angles. These tripods allow you to hang your camera rather than mounting it.

Whether you're using video for communication, marketing, or both, there is a wide range of options available to you when it comes to film production. You can produce excellent videos with a very simple setup. You can also choose to explore some subtle details that can continue to level up your video production. The options are limitless, but the choice is ultimately yours.

RECORDING YOUR VIDEO

You have all the tools in place. Now it is time to hit "Record." What do you need to do? Do a quick test recording to ensure your frame looks the way you want it to look. Make sure your recording includes sound because you want to check to ensure the sound is connected to the proper recording devices.[32] After your review, you can begin recording. A more detailed recording checklist is available in Chapter 11.

Suppose you are recording a standard talking head video. After you hit the "Start Recording" button, pause for 3 to 5 seconds. This step will allow you to have room to edit the beginning of the clip with greater ease. You may even have room for a transition video at the beginning. Pace yourself. Pacing not only helps your potential clients understand your message more clearly, but it also can help you in the editing process.

Regarding editing, what can you do when recording if you make a mistake? Well, pause for a few seconds, 10 to 20 seconds, and see if it is possible to go back to the beginning of the point you are currently explaining. During the editing process, you may find that it will be easier than you think to cut out that portion of your video.

Another question regarding recording is often whether you need to read from a teleprompter. The answer to this question is that it depends on your style. There are positives and negatives to both options. Some prefer to read from a carefully written and edited script uploaded to a teleprompter. However, many people work

[31] PHOPIK 77 Camera Tripod, Travel Tripod for DSLR, Professional Tripod with 360 Degree Ball Head, Camera Tripods & Monopods with Carry Bag for Camera, Ipad, Phone, Lightweight Load up to 17.6 Pounds.

[32] "8 Step Checklist for Filming (BEFORE You Hit Record)," *Primal Video*, n.d., www.primalvideo.com/video-creation/shooting/ultimate-checklist-for-filming/.

from a loose outline. You could also write out a script and memorize it. We discuss the development of your script in Chapter 10. There are no definitive rules. The goal should be great authentic content that resonates. In other words, choose authenticity over perfection.

If you work with a teleprompter, you can know exactly what to say because you have already decided on word choice and language. That being said, if you are using a teleprompter, your audience should not be able to tell. In other words, you want to avoid sounding robotic and inauthentic. Mastery of the teleprompter requires practice, and this option will need you to spend time writing out your script. If you prefer this method, there is a broad spectrum of possibilities at your disposal from a software perspective.

The tool that you use is in part dependent upon what your main recording device is. If you are recording a video using your phone, there are a few apps you can download that serve as a teleprompter while you record. One of the most popular teleprompter apps in this category is the BIGVU application.[33] Copy and paste your script into the app, hit "Record," and read your words as they roll across the top of your phone screen. BIGVU also offers options for AI script generation, easy editing, styled captions, and one-click social media posting.[34] BIGVU offers a limited free version of the app as well as paid tier levels with more features.[35]

If you are recording into your computer, there are websites designed to serve as teleprompters. The challenge with some of these websites is that because they call your attention to the screen below the camera, the direction of your gaze might not be ideal for video. Your viewers might be able to tell that you are reading a script. To avoid that, consider teleprompter tools and applications that turn your tablet or cell phone into a teleprompter. Many of these tools are paired with specific apps recommended by the manufacturers.

These teleprompter setups are best used in situations where the subject reading from the teleprompter will not be too far away and is able to read the smaller screen. For more instances where the subject will be further you may need a standalone device with a larger screen. Some of these teleprompter kits also include additional accessories like Bluetooth remote controls and storage cases. The prices for these different setups vary depending on the size of the screen, ease of setup, and the accompanying accessories.

---

[33] BIGVU, www.bigvu.tv.

[34] Ibid.

[35] Pricing options, BIGVU, n.d., bigvu.tv/pricing.

My personal preferred method is the use of an outline. I found that I could decrease prep time and communicate authentically with an outline. As a result, when recording, I post my outline to a whiteboard in the background or use my iPad for quick referencing. Using a script is difficult to sort through mentally as I focus on communicating value to my potential and current clients. Regardless of your selected method, the outlines you develop in Chapter 10 should provide a solid foundation for your video.

Finally, when it comes to editing simple videos, keep it simple. Avoid trying to do too much. Consider using native editing apps on your phone or the tools built into your computer. Simply cut out the initial seconds of the video. Your videos may be reasonably simple, but if the content is solid and straightforward, that will be sufficient.

ADDITIONAL CONSIDERATIONS

Your Posture

Your posture can affect the way you look on camera because it impacts the angles you are working with. If you lean toward the camera too close, the camera will emphasize your face's natural angles and shadows in strange ways. However, you may appear wide if you are too far from the camera because you are leaning back in your chair. Photographer Gia Goodrich recommends having a small pillow positioned at your back to help you produce the correct posture for Zoom.[36]

Creating a Dedicated Space

Bulk Create

Consider having a dedicated space curated for creating your videos. A dedicated space can allow you to have your setup with your camera, lighting, and sound structure so that you are not required to build up and tear down each time. If that is not an option for you, consider identifying a specific time set aside for the bulk creation of your videos.

In the past, I've aimed to have one content recording day per month or quarter depending on my schedule. To do this, I would select a date and time when I had a few hours to record multiple videos. I then would usually record two or three videos in the same outfit (and my community never seems to mind).

All in all, with these tools you can create quality videos in most of the formats we discussed.

---

[36] Gia Goodrich, "How to Look Better on Zoom [How to Light & Angle Your Screen to Look Your Best]," YouTube video, 10:52, uploaded April 30, 2020, https://www.youtube.com/watch?v=YO6utfQm7Bg.

PART 2

Video for Communications

As a new lawyer, I was fascinated by the entrepreneurial attorneys who discovered ways to create "virtual practices." These were law firms that did not operate in traditional brick-and-mortar structures. Instead, these law firms discovered ways to find clients and serve them using their computers and ingenuity. I wanted to be like them. As a result, I sought out information on how these law firms ran. One key component for all of them was the use of video conferences.

WHAT IS A VIDEO CONFERENCE?

Video conferencing, at its core, is using video to connect with one or more people. There are no fixed rules regarding what is considered video conferencing, but in today's world, video conferencing is used to describe one-to-one meetings and meetings where multiple people in one room are conferring with one or more people in another location via video.

After the coronavirus pandemic, most attorneys have had at least an initial introduction to video conferencing; however, you may not have made it part of your firm's daily practice. There are also many legal professionals who are already using it in some capacity but want to learn how to use it more effectively. Regardless of your experience, it is important to acknowledge that video conferencing offers tremendous benefits to attorneys, their staff members, and most importantly, their clients. Two significant benefits include

- **Flexibility**. By offering video conferencing in your firm, you create opportunities for your firm to connect with ease. This ease increases the ability to respond swiftly.
- **Authenticity**. Video conferencing makes it easier to communicate with your clients and have them authentically share with you. Because you are speaking face-to-face, the ability to fake something or deceive is reduced. The same nonverbal cues provided in person can be conveyed and transmitted through video calls.

Part 2 focuses on the use of video for communication with a particular focus on its use through video conferencing. We will start by addressing common mistakes people make during these calls. Then I will provide recommendations for best practices and tools to use.

4

Common Video Conferencing Mistakes

> "Can we ask participants to mute unless they are speaking? Unless Kevin is a presenter, I don't need to hear his random sounds or see his screen featured."

The DM was sent to me discreetly in the middle of one of my marathon Zoom days, and I completely understood the participant's frustration. Every time Kevin agreed with something a main presenter said, we would be notified with his approving sigh or mumbled agreement interjected into the Zoom room atmosphere and his green highlighted box. Although Kevin seemed like a great person, this minor annoyance did not bode well for the overall impression he left on his fellow meeting participants.

And he had no idea.

I imagine you probably have your own story of some awkward or annoying experience you have had with a fellow video conference participant that impaired your ability to enjoy or engage in the meeting. You remember how distracting those behaviors were and how your mind wandered in annoyance. Mistakes like distracting visuals and sounds undermine the professional tone that you need to convey when video conferencing. As we begin our conversation on video conferencing, let's review the most common video conferencing mistakes you might be making.

DISTRACTING VISUALS

At the height of the COVID-19 pandemic, video conferencing fails were all over social media and the news. Every other video highlighted someone who forgot they were in the middle of a video conference and carried out some awkward or embarrassing behavior. The origin of these embarrassing stories stems from the distracting activities video conference participants were known to engage in.

Now your video conference faux pas probably will not go viral (and in this case, that's a good thing). Still, you may gain negative popularity in your organization or community if you have distracting visuals.

What Constitutes a Distracting Visual?

I consider visual elements distracting if they draw the meeting participants' attention away from the intended focal point during the meeting. These may be instances where there is too much movement, an awkward camera angle, or strange backgrounds.

You may be wondering, does this matter? Well, I would like to propose an alternative approach. Rather than considering whether the distraction is a big deal, ask yourself how important the subject matter at hand is. Why conduct the video conference if it's not important enough to warrant your attention?

I am reminded of advice I received as a law student preparing for on-campus interviews with various firms and organizations. I was wearing one of my favorite pairs of dangly earrings. My advisor provided guidance on how to dress for these interviews. She said, "Your personality is important, but when you are in an interview, your message is most important. You don't want to underdress or overdress in a way that distracts your audience from actually hearing and experiencing you."

That conversation was so eye opening because it made me realize that distractions can also encompass things that would be positive in some contexts—like those conversation piece earrings—yet could draw attention away from the business of your video conference. As I've thought about that advice over the years, I have considered what I want to communicate in my interactions. It is sometimes appropriate/beneficial to have visual focal points that speak on your behalf, but we will address how to do that in Chapter 8. For now, consider how you may be distracting your audience with poor visuals.

In one of the most distracting visual behaviors, one person in the meeting carries the phone with the meeting on it while walking around their office. Whether they are the main speaker or not, the motion is dizzying and has a way of drawing the audience's attention. Instead of listening to the person who has the floor, they wonder, "Where is she going?" or "Can't he sit still?"

In another example, the person seems to strategically position their laptop on their lap. Placing their laptop there during a video conference creates an unsightly view of that person's belly, nose, or chest instead of their face. In these instances, you can correct this by raising the laptop on some books, so the camera is at eye level, tilting the laptop, or using a mount. Consider the same changes if you are using your phone and desire to reposition the camera's angle.

These two examples give the impression that you are disorganized or in a chaotic environment or situation. In a business setting, it's best to make sure your setup is organized and ready before you sign on to a video conference—or, when that isn't possible, simply excuse yourself from having your camera on until you are in a place/situation where you are settled in one place.

Another example of a distracting visual is the individual who is clearly on their phone, either speaking or texting. This is most apparent during video conferences with fewer participants. Often, the individual does not think anyone can see them, but it is obvious to others on the call. This distraction is exacerbated when the culprit requests information that was shared earlier, while they were distracted. If you must take a call or respond to a text message, it may be more appropriate to turn off your camera for a moment. Otherwise, don't take the call and let it go to voicemail until the videoconference is over.

We have all found ourselves glancing at our devices occasionally, but this can be highly detrimental when attempting to establish an authentic connection with your potential client or instill a culture of trust and respect within your team.

Another source of distraction can be your background. Here are a few examples of distractions in your background:

- Having other people moving in the background
- A virtual background creating a strange halo effect that makes your face or head appear disconnected from your body
- Joining a virtual meeting from a bedroom
- Joining a virtual meeting from a very cluttered room

Unless your actual background is inappropriate (too much activity or too disorganized), use your natural background to ensure that your audience is not distracted. You may also use the "blur my background" feature available with some video conferencing software. We discuss additional ways to improve your background in Chapter 8.

DISTRACTING SOUNDS

Sound can be another source of distraction during video conferences. The distraction may come in the form of strange background noises or simply poor audio functions or settings. These distractions are often unintentional but can create some of the most significant video conference disruptions. Kevin's story at the beginning of the chapter is a perfect example of the impact of distracting sounds.

Some examples include leaving your sound unmuted while typing with intensity (or typing at all). The sound of your fingers clacking against the keyboard can often be heard, creating distractions for those attempting to listen to the speaker. This distraction can also occur when you are responding with light commentary. In an in-person setting, this might not be as distracting. A few "mhm's" and "Right's" would be unremarkable and perhaps even welcome. However, these noises can make it difficult for the audience and the individual presenting in a virtual environment to hear or concentrate.

If a conference participant has multiple output devices near each other, this can create distracting audio. For example, it is common to have people join calls using two devices: their cellphone and their laptop. In these instances, the audio creates an echo and terrible feedback. Sometimes, a speaker may try to speak over the feedback, but the best solution is to disconnect one of the audio sources.

You can also preempt this issue when you introduce the second device. Platforms like Zoom prompt you to choose one of the audio conference options when you are joining a meeting. In such cases, do not join the meeting with audio. This will result in your initial meeting source serving as your sole audio source. Additional technical distractions can occur if a computer or laptop fan runs loudly in the background. When you cannot change your hardware, try to close out some of the concurrent applications or windows.

The best rule is to stay muted unless and until you speak. This is standard practice and will be appreciated by those on the video conference with you. If you are hosting the video conference, you may have the option to mute everyone as necessary. You can also set your audio and meeting preferences to have participants automatically muted upon entry.

VIDEO CONFERENCES THAT ARE TOO FREQUENT OR TOO LONG

It may seem strange in a book about video to talk about limiting the number of video conferences you conduct, but too many video conferences can be unproductive. There is such a thing as too many video conferences.

How do you know if you have too many video conferences?

- Do you find it challenging to find time to do any of the actual work that comes from these meetings?
- Are your clients or team members frequently disengaged during your video conferences?
- Can a decision replace the need for this meeting and are you empowered to make that decision?

If you answered yes to any of these questions, you might be making the mistake of having too many video conferences.

Not only is it unproductive to hold too many video conferences, but video conferences that are too long can also result in diminishing returns. "Diminishing returns" is an economic concept that says, "after some optimal level of capacity is reached, adding an additional factor of production will actually result in smaller increases in output."[1] An example of this is a meeting scheduled for a team that has a pressing deadline, causing the team stress. A longer meeting at this time may simply increase stress and decrease productivity.

I am particularly passionate about this as a former educator. When we examine the best practices for productivity, learning, collaboration, and many of the things we desire to see when we conduct meetings, the research suggests taking frequent breaks and holding shorter meetings.[2] Ironically, it seems that as our attention spans decrease, we are holding longer and longer virtual meetings. Devoting too much time to video conferences—whether scheduling them too often or letting them go on for too long—results in diminishing returns.

This phenomenon was so prevalent during the COVID-19 lockdown that the term "Zoom fatigue" became a point of discussion. Zoom fatigue "describe[s] the

[1] Adam Hayes, "Law of Diminishing Marginal Returns: Definition, Example, Use in Economics," *Investopedia*, n.d., https://www.investopedia.com/terms/l/lawofdiminishingmarginalreturn.asp.

[2] Salman Khan, "Why Long Lectures Are Ineffective," *Time*, October 2, 2012, https://ideas.time.com/2012/10/02/why-lectures-are-ineffective/#:~:text=Students%20remembered%20far%20more%20of,unapplied%20in%20the%20real%20world.

tiredness, anxiety, or worry resulting from overusing these virtual platforms.[3] In 2021, Stanford University professors examined the impact of spending excessive time in video conferences.[4] The research concluded that video conferencing requires much eye contact, and engagement with screens in this manner creates unnatural intensity. This intensity can trigger increased social anxiety, particularly in women who are socialized to be more aware of the way they visually appear.[5]

As a product of today's world, I have struggled with long meetings in person and virtual from my days as a student at the University of Georgia. I performed notably better during courses that did not exceed 50 minutes, whereas I struggled in my courses that required more prolonged periods of focus. I found that when we exceeded the 1-hour point, I would disengage. In classes where I managed to stay present, I still desired time to process the information I received before layering it with additional details. As a result, I tend to encourage breaks in longer video conferences at least once around the 50-minute mark.

Be very intentional about how frequent and how long these meetings are. It may be helpful to implement days or blocks of time that are protected from virtual conferences. Additionally, allow for times when the video does not have to be on. By inviting this type of flexibility, you are allowing participants to engage in ways that are not taxing. Practices like this also use less bandwidth on your team's computers resulting in less jitters and lag.

By being selective about the frequency and length of these meetings, you are honoring your time and teaching others, whether your team or your potential clients, to do the same.

LACK OF PREPARATION

Another problem that can significantly undermine the success of your video conference is the lack of preparation. Due to the increased ease and convenience associated with hosting Zoom calls and virtual presentations, a common theme is for people to forgo common meeting preparation etiquette. Participants enter their

---

[3] Carolyn Reinach Wolf, "Virtual Platforms Are Helpful Tools but Can Add to Our Stress," *Psychology Today*, May 14, 2020, https://www.psychologytoday.com/us/blog/the-desk-the-mental-health-lawyer/202005/virtual-platforms-are-helpful-tools-can-add-our-stress.

[4] "Stanford Researchers Identify Four Causes for 'Zoom Fatigue' and Their Simple Fixes," *Stanford Report*, February 23, 2021, https://news.stanford.edu/2021/02/23/four-causes-zoom-fatigue-solutions/.

[5] "Zoom Fatigue Worse for Women, Stanford Study Finds," *Stanford Report*, April 13, 2021, https://news.stanford.edu/2021/04/13/zoom-fatigue-worse-women.

virtual conferences with a broad topic in mind but no specific agenda or intended objective for a meeting.

Without an agenda, there is no plan to dictate how that time is spent. As a recovering procrastinator, I was guilty of this practice. I would log on to meetings with team members only to spend the first 10 to 15 minutes trying to figure out our primary goal for the call. I would feel terrible each time because, without a fixed plan, we often ended the meeting with more questions than answers. Additionally, I was paying my team members for these calls without stated objectives. It was ridiculous.

So, I had to change my ways.

I implemented a standard plan we would use every time we met. My virtual meeting agendas include time for us to review firm objectives and for the team members to ask me any questions. The results have been terrific. My team was re-engaged and came to each meeting knowing exactly how to prepare because they had access to the agenda in advance. Implementing the standard plan and agenda made a significant difference in the effectiveness of those meetings.

Another sign of a lack of preparation is a technological failure. One organization I participated in had a frequent issue where its facilitators repeatedly faced the same issues week after week because a lack of preparation persisted. This lack of preparation resulted in fewer and fewer attendees each week because participants were frustrated with the consistent issues with logging on to the selected platform. The standard message "waiting for host to start" seemed to plague their programs.

When technology is inadequately tested, the audience is unable to engage appropriately. Additionally, a speaker who may have spent time preparing material may be thrown off due to the lack of technology.

I recall a situation when I was traveling but was required to provide a short presentation for a volunteer organization I assist with. Upon logging in to the Zoom room approximately 1 minute before start time, I assumed I could easily navigate the system on my backup tool. I was wrong. As I attempted to share my screen, I realized my plan was flawed. I did not know how to share my screen using the iPad. This inability to use the tools I set up left me frustrated and disappointed in the quality of my presentation.

This did not have to be the case. After logging off the call, I did the testing I should have done earlier and discovered that a few simple clicks would provide the opportunity I needed to share the screen and distinguish my presentation.

As a meeting host you can avoid several technological problems by conducting a private run-through. Log in to your video conferencing platform using the device you plan on using during the actual call. Additionally, try to arrive on the video platform a few minutes before the start of the meeting to ensure that everything is running smoothly. Check the following items before your call:

- Check to make sure your internet connection is actually on.
- Check your video source to make sure the appropriate camera is detected and on.
- Check your audio source to make sure the appropriate microphone is detected on.
- If you are using headphones, check to make sure the software has properly detected your headphones as the audio output source.
- Check your background to make sure all settings are correct and that all filters (especially cat filters 😉) are off.

INAPPROPRIATE TONE

Another mistake that impacts our video conferences is not setting the appropriate tone. This particular mistake is more nuanced than the others and requires consideration of several factors.

Essentially, there are times during your video conferences when imposing an overly professional tone could undermine the success of the overall meeting and vice versa. For example, there are instances where team leaders and firm owners attempt to impose strict formal requirements over virtual conferences regarding participation or attire that cannot be appropriately enforced, given the nature of the platforms. When these leaders take steps to try to impose these mandates, team members and audience members are more likely to disengage from the meeting.

The same can be said when formal conversations are approached from an informal perspective. For example, during initial consultations with clients, my practice is to encourage professionalism from the attorney's staff to establish the importance and seriousness of the work in question. That being said, we may find that there are instances where the attorney maintains that sense of professionalism while showing grace toward clients who may not be able to accommodate the same level of professionalism due to unique personal situations.

CONCLUSION

The mistakes discussed in this chapter are not by any means exhaustive. However, these mistakes can significantly impair your video conferences and how your audience receives you. Many of these activities convey a sense of irresponsibility that does not support healthy perceptions of who you are as an attorney.

More importantly, these actions have the potential consequence of closing off your ability to connect with your intended audiences.

Now that we have examined a few common mistakes, we will spend the next few chapters discussing how to conduct video conferences so that you can incorporate video conferencing successfully with staff members and clients or potential clients.

5

Video Conferencing with Staff

> "Clients do not come first. Employees come first. If you take care of your employees, they will take care of the clients."[1]
>
> —Richard Branson, founder of the Virgin Group

When it comes to revolutionizing your firm with video and enhancing your practice, you cannot overlook the role of video with your staff. In this chapter, we will explore how to effectively incorporate video into your firm's culture without eroding the professionalism of your practice.

Your team is the backbone of your law firm, and the way you communicate with them impacts every aspect of your firm. In incorporating video conferencing into your firm, it is critical to remember that the use of video should support an already healthy culture of communication and further support your relationship with your team.

Additionally, before we dive into discussing the different types of meetings you can implement via video conferencing, it is important to discuss the role of

[1] Marcel Schwantes, "It Took Richard Branson a Few Words to Teach the Best Leadership Lesson You Will Hear Today," *Inc.*, February 26, 2018, https://www.inc.com/marcel-schwantes/it-took-richard-branson-a-few-words-to-teach-best-leadership-lesson-you-will-hear-today.html.

leadership in establishing communication practices, systems, and vision for your firm. My philosophy to effective video conferencing as a communicative tool is built around an in-depth understanding of what it means to lead.

John C. Maxwell defines leadership as influence.[2] Thus, in this context as a law firm owner, you are the primary influence on your team. As the primary leader in the practice, it is essential to cast the vision for your firm. Vision can be defined as "the dream and the direction for your company. It's what forms your company culture, guides your decisions, and helps you set—and crush—your goals. It's what inspires others to follow you, work hard and make a difference."[3]

In the context of video conferencing and overall communications, you then are responsible for setting the direction for what you would like those communications to look and sound like. You get to determine the culture and tenor of your meetings. In instances when you are not leading the meeting, your expectations, and the culture you have envisioned and taught should be replicated by your team. This is especially true when you take on the "leadership is influence" mindset and commit to helping others become leaders too.

It is possible and practical that other forms of leadership exist within your organization. Depending on your team's size and makeup, different people will likely function as a leader at different times—and this is a very good thing. Viewing leadership from this more expansive lens allows you to empower your team to collaborate with greater effectiveness.

Additionally, if we apply this leadership lens to video conferencing, even in times when an individual may not be formally tasked with the leadership of a video conference, if leadership is in fact influence, we can outline how they can contribute, prepare, and influence even as participants.

The practices we encourage in this video conferencing chapter are designed to help you lead more effectively and inspire others in your organization to do the same.

BENEFITS OF USING VIDEO TO COMMUNICATE INTERNALLY

There are several benefits associated with using video in your law firm for both you and your staff. One of the primary benefits of incorporating video is that it

---

[2] "How to Gain Influence (Part 1)," *The John Maxwell Leadership Podcast*, February 9, 2022, https://johnmaxwellleadershippodcast.com/episodes/john-maxwell-how-to-gain-influence-1#:~:text=John%20Maxwell%20says%20that%20leadership,leadership%20with%20those%20you%20lead.

[3] Tony Robbins, "How to Build Your Leadership Vision," *Tony Robbins Official Website*, n.d., https://www.tonyrobbins.com/what-is-leadership/leadership-vision/#:~:text=Business%20Identity%20Quiz-,What%20is%20vision%20in%20leadership%3F,hard%20and%20make%20a%20difference.

provides greater flexibility for staff members. Unlike in the past, by combining video, you can provide more ways for your staff to work. You may be able to create hybrid or entirely virtual positions. Additionally, for you as an employer, video can create opportunities to recruit talent from a wider pool of applicants. You are no longer limited to finding workers in your immediate location. As I built my practice, I knew it was time to find additional help. I created job openings in various locations. However, one individual who reached out to me was a young woman from Nigeria. She stood out and provided excellent work. And personally, it was even more meaningful to me as a first-generation Nigerian American. The use of virtual conferencing made that possible. I was not bound to my immediate network.

Please note that while your recruitment pool can be expanded, ethical issues regarding what constitutes the practice of law and the unauthorized practice of law in various states should be considered. Check your jurisdiction's rules to ensure that you remain in compliance.

TYPES OF INTERNAL TEAM MEETINGS APPROPRIATE FOR VIDEO COMMUNICATION

The key to effective video conferences is creating the right type of team meetings. Books like *Traction: Get a Grip on Your Business*[4] and *Mastering the Rockefeller Habits*[5] all refer to the impact of effective team meetings. However, for these meetings to be leveled up, they must be effective irrespective of the channel. The following are seven types of meetings that can be conducted effectively via video:

- Quarterly/Monthly All-Staff Meetings
- Case Strategy Meetings
- Weekly Check-In Meetings
- Daily Check-In Meetings
- Training Meetings
- Performance Review Meetings
- Weekly Department Meetings

Two factors that will significantly influence the types of meetings you hold are your practice area and the size of your firm. Let's look at each of these meetings one at a time.

---

[4] Gino Wickman, *Traction: Get a Grip on Your Business* (BenBella Books, 2012).

[5] Verne Harnish, *Mastering the Rockefeller Habits: What You Must Do to Increase the Value of Your Growing Firm* (Gazelles, 2002).

All-Staff Meetings

An all-staff meeting is a regularly scheduled meeting required for all workers. As your team grows, keeping everyone aligned and informed regarding the firm's priorities and key objectives becomes more challenging. Your all-staff meeting should involve telling team members what the company is up to and how major goals will be tackled. This is also an opportunity to reinforce positive company behaviors and correct negative ones. The frequency of these meetings will vary depending on the size of your firm. Smaller firms with 2 to 8 people can have weekly all-staff meetings, whereas law firms with 10 to 20 team members may find that monthly or biweekly meetings may be preferred.

Case Strategy Meetings

Another meeting you may find beneficial to conduct via video conferencing is the case strategy meeting. A case strategy meeting is designed to get work done on your engaged client matters. During this meeting, depending on the firm's size and practice area, the case strategy meeting may be the perfect arena in which to brainstorm potential strategies with other team members.

One key thing to keep in mind during case strategy meetings is that they should be action oriented. By action oriented I mean that this meeting should lead to meaning decisions and actions that move your cases forward. A common trap I see many fall into with strategy meetings is that at the end of the conversation, decisions are deferred, even though all the information and insights needed have been provided. Avoid this trap. Be decisive when it is time to be decisive.

Check-In Meetings

I believe every team member should have the opportunity to speak with a supervisor at least once a week to bring clarity to projects and ensure that goals are still aligned. You may find yourself implementing weekly department meetings in your firm, if your business has grown to a level at which you have various people working on different segments of the firm. The goal of the weekly department meeting is to facilitate collaboration and help team leaders stay informed regarding the work being completed.

These weekly check-ins give teammates opportunities to collaborate truly and troubleshoot problems in advance. If your legal team is significantly large, you likely will not be able to have a one-to-one encounter with each team member, but you should ensure that someone is able to have that meeting with them.

As you build out your internal video conferencing systems, maintain consistency by scheduling these meetings for the same day and time each week. Many of the popular organizational calendaring tools have integrations that make it easy to access the virtual rooms. Additionally, consider having a preset template agenda that outlines the things you would like to discuss each week with your team.

During my time with WealthCounsel, one of our vice presidents implemented a common practice known as a huddle before the initiative became a company-wide practice. These were the rules of our huddles:

1. The last person to join the call would be the first person to give their huddle.
2. Each person was required to share their top three accomplishments from the past week and the three priorities for the week.
3. Then the person would share any hurdles, roadblocks, or impediments to the success of their stated priorities.
4. Finally, we were each required to share a win, and that win was not limited to merely professional successes.

Because of the nature of the individuals on the team and these weekly meetings, our team had significant cohesion. We learned about one another and collaborated. These huddles allowed us to stay focused on our objectives while building healthy interdependent relationships with one another.

One key item on the agenda for your virtual check-ins should be addressing batched questions. Batching questions is the process of gathering the nonemergency, yet important questions that come up over the course of the day and asking about them at a specific time. This allows for more continuity in the workday and can be immensely helpful to keep everyone's interruptions limited. This batching allows these meetings to keep you connected to what your team members are doing without breaking their focus.

Team members also benefit from this meeting because their questions are being answered. You should keep your check-in meetings to a reasonable length to ensure full engagement and attention. You should also incorporate the use of an ongoing agenda that allows you to make sure you keep focused on your prize. Using a plan helps you and your team focus throughout the process.

That being said, just because you are the firm's leader does not mean that meetings with you are required to be cold, sterile, or rigid. Approaching video conference calls (and in-person) meetings like this will likely limit your influence and impact. Your team is more likely to respond positively to you if you can become someone who allows them to bring their best selves to the meeting. To combat a sterile environment, allow your personality to shine and show genuine interest in the person on the other side of the screen.

Additionally, during your meetings, you are best positioned to create buy-in to the firm vision. Buy-in is critical when connecting with your team because their buy-in to your vision allows them to provide better service as a direct result of the belief present. The late Maya Angelou said, "I've learned that people will forget what you said, people will forget what you did, but people will never forget how you made them feel."[6] President Theodore Roosevelt said, "Nobody cares how much you know until they know how much you care."[7] During your meetings with team members you are able to show that you care by taking time to ask about their lives. You can maintain professionalism and display empathy at the same time.

A Word on Daily Check-In Meetings

Daily check-ins are meetings designed to help teams stay connected and aware regarding what other team members are working on. This could also look like a quick 5-minute video meeting within a small team or department to hear everyone's priorities for the day. If you are a solo or small firm owner, this may look like a meeting with your assistant briefly at the start of each week to make sure priorities are aligned.

Training Meetings

Another important type of video conference you can have with your team are meetings intended to provide training. The great thing about utilizing video for training is that you can record exactly what you do for your staff. When using this type of meeting, the recording allows you to document what you have communicated to your team member.

One prime example of using videos to train is during onboarding. When bringing a new team member on, an onboarding video series could help introduce your new hire to important people in the firm, provide insight into the technological tools used, and provide a roadmap of how to access important resources within the firm. You can also use these videos to introduce and reinforce cultural norms and values you want to establish in your firm.

---

[6] Bob Glaves, "People Remember How You Made Them Feel," *Chicago Bar Foundation*, n.d., www.chicagobarfoundation.org/bobservations/people-remember-made-feel/.

[7] "Theodore Roosevelt Quotes," *Theodore Roosevelt Center at Dickinson State University*, www.theodorerooseveltcenter.org/Learn-About-TR/TR-Quotes?page=112.

When developing training material, such as onboarding content, remember your audience. Training content should be developed in a step-by-step approach. I have found that training material is particularly helpful when used to show a team member how to navigate a commonly used tool in the firm. It may be helpful to have a corresponding written database that accompanies videos. This database should include links to software or tools used and additional resources for more help if needed.

Another thing to keep in mind when developing videos for training is length. Surprisingly, staring into a computer screen can be extremely draining. Break down training videos into smaller pieces of content so that it is more manageable for your team members to digest. Additionally, if they have to return to the training materials for clarification, they will not be forced to sift through large portions of video.

If you are providing training in substantive legal areas, this information is still just as relevant. Substantive law can be dense. Creating videos that simplify content can make a huge difference in how well your team members process the information.

To enhance engagement, particularly for onboarding purposes, consider making the videos interactive by asking team members to do some type of activity to show their understanding. It may be a short quiz created on a survey platform. Be open and creative.

Finally, there is no hard-and-fast rule about who should record the video. The goal is to provide the information in a clear, easy-to-understand format. If another team member can explain the concept or process in a succinct manner, they can be entrusted to record the video. The only content that I would say should be created by leadership is content that speaks to the vision, culture, and values of the firm. For the most part, other content can be deferred to someone else if someone else is available to create it.

Performance Review Meetings

Performance review meetings allow you to meet with your team members to discuss their how well they are performing their job or tasks. These meetings should occur at least twice a year, but quarterly meetings are also feasible. Use this time to focus on where this team member is successful, where they have room for improvement, and devising a plan for continued growth and success.

These meetings are particularly important to conduct via video or in person because they often involve telling people about areas of improvement. Different people may receive feedback differently, so you want to be able to provide clarity and answer questions regarding how you determined the findings on your reviews. This will also allow you to gather important feedback about your team by providing an opportunity for you to see and interpret their body language.

Remember, with performance reviews, you should be highlighting the positive so that you can encourage your team member to continue the behavior, and addressing areas of improvement clearly so that your team member has an opportunity to improve.

Department Meetings

Finally, consider implementing department meetings focused on establishing clear alignment between a team's function and the overall organizational goals. These meetings should occur at least once a month to ensure clarity for every part of your team.

As you meet with your team, consider ways to use the technology to create a shared experience. You should also consider ways to add more visual elements. Some companies require team members to have their cameras on during meetings. A rule like this encourages participation but consider providing flexibility with this rule. In instances where there are many video conferences, allow for sessions when having video on is not required. As discussed earlier, Zoom fatigue is real, and the need to keep cameras on throughout further enhances the adverse effects associated with this phenomenon.

USING VIDEO TO DOCUMENT SYSTEMS IN YOUR FIRM

So far in this chapter, we have been exploring the use of video to communicate within your firm, but before we cover software and tools, I wanted to point out one more way you can use video internally. You can use video to improve processes and systems by improving documentation. The benefits of video internally are not limited to meetings alone.

One of the most common challenges solo and small law firm leaders face when it comes to communicating and connecting is documentation. Information and knowledge are lost in transit after conversations and video conferences, leading to inefficiency and frustration. But video can help fix that.

Video documentation is simple to create. With the technology available today through our phones, tablets, and computers, it does not require high levels of skill or effort. Additionally, certain ideas and concepts are more clearly received when provided via video. Finally, because of the easy access you can create, this may help you to scale up your team's efforts more quickly.

One reason why I wanted to include this content here is because much of your documentation can be created while you are carrying out the work. To better depict this, consider the training meetings we described earlier. Many video tools include the option to record your screen so that you walk your team through each step. Then if they have a question about something, they can refer to the video to troubleshoot it on their own.

By recording conversations where vital concepts are explained or new processes are introduced, you are creating a record that can be referenced in the future if any additional questions arise. The video record can also be used as the first step in troubleshooting problems that may occur as team members attempt to replicate the processes you have created in your firm.

Your team can reuse these videos to continue to train your workforce as you grow. The videos you record can be used by other teammates. Even the most complex legal area has some simple, repeatable tasks.

You can use those videos to create an onboarding video library that introduces the worker to the law firm. This is particularly helpful when your staff needs to use new software they might not be accustomed to. You can also choose to enhance these videos. You may decide to add things like text, figures, diagrams, and photos to your videos, making them even more engaging and helpful to those who watch them.

As an attorney assisting business owners in the formation of their businesses and the registration of their intellectual property, as well as one who served as a legal mentor for a nationally recognized company, many of the tasks I completed involved repeated processes. I found that to decrease the use of my time on administrative tasks, I needed to provide visual aids easily accessible without my direct involvement. So, I began creating video libraries.

My process was very simple. If a team member asked a question about something, I would use one of the video conferencing tools like Zoom to record that portion of our conversation. If annotations were needed, I would use the annotation or smart board feature in Zoom. In other instances, I would use other tools to record my screen.

My go-to tool for documentation has been Loom.[8] Loom is a video communication tool designed to help you quickly record, edit, and share video and screen

[8] "That Meeting Should Have Been a Loom Video," *Loom*, n.d., https://www.loom.com/.

shares with your audience. Like Zoom, Loom experienced explosive growth during the early stages of the pandemic. At the time of this writing, Loom's website invites users to "Show it, say it, send it." Loom requires a Google Chrome plug-in.

One positive aspect of Loom is the easy ability to switch cameras. Once the plug-in is installed, with a quick click of a button, you can record a video of your entire screen or one tab of your browser. You can also choose to record pure video without any screen elements.

Additionally, Loom allows you to record videos that your viewer can engage with. Viewers can leave time-stamped comments. If your viewers do not want to leave comments, they can leave reactions in the form of emojis. Loom also has the option of creating subtitles. With subtitles, your training videos will augment viewers' understanding of what you are teaching. Along those same lines, if there are questions about something, your team can refer to the Loom library to access the video. To take your training videos to the next level on Loom, consider adding a call to action that links to a corresponding quiz to ensure viewers understand the concepts you are demonstrating.

In my role as Practice Success Mentor for WealthCounsel, one of my favorite experiences involved a client requesting feedback on a tool she was developing for her clients. One of the tools I incorporated in providing that service to her was Loom. She recorded her initial request via Loom, and I was able to send a direct video response.

Both video creation tools like Loom and Zoom offer features such as screen recording, video commenting, reactions, and subtitles to make interactive videos for training and communication. While Zoom provides some overlapping functionality, Loom is purpose-built for asynchronous video with viewer engagement in mind.

Another screen recording alternative is Camtasia.[9] Camtasia is a robust screen recording and video editing software that allows you to add engaging elements to your videos.

When evaluating tools, look for time-stamped comments to pinpoint feedback, emoji reactions to gauge sentiment, automatic subtitles for accessibility, and options to link training videos to quizzes. The key is choosing a tool that enables the kind of video interactivity that suits your needs.

---

[9] "The Best All-in-One Screen Recorder and Video Editor," *TechSmith Camtasia*, n.d., https://discover.techsmith.com/camtasia-gs-us/.

BEST PRACTICES FOR VIDEO CONFERENCING WITH YOUR TEAM

As you consider the best ways to connect with your team via video conferencing, there are a few best practices. By exploring these elements, you can ensure that video conferencing takes your firm to the next level.

Establishing Norms

First, it is essential to establish norms or ground rules regarding your video conferences. What type of conduct is allowed via video conferences? Are there some video conferences where cameras must be on? If you are working with remote staff, are there specific times off-limits? Consider these various elements as you establish norms for your law firm that support the culture you intend to create and prepare your team to be fully present for the other work they will be required to carry out.

Another element of establishing norms is selecting specific times when you will meet. Along the same lines, consider different time zones. Some periods are ideal for you and your team members without significantly infringing on another member's daily rhythms.

Finally, consider how and when you bring up conflicts during your virtual meetings. The popular corporate Instagram influencer known as @therealveronika_ went viral in 2024 for a skit depicting a leader's inconsistency with team members online.[10] In the skit, the leader was prepared to highlight an assumed shortcoming of one teammate, but quickly retracted when she discovered that the root issue was another team member who had to be her friend. The funny but insightful clip highlights how inconsistencies in addressing issues can erode trust between team members and undermine a leader's authority, so establish boundaries regarding what is addressed publicly and privately and be consistent with your choice.

Use an Agenda

One easily overlooked tool that can improve your video conferences with team members is the use of an agenda. An agenda allows you to set the stage for your team's expectations during the meeting. By having a clear agenda, you can ensure

[10] Veronika Rivera (@therealveronika_), "We're gonna talk about it NOW," TikTok posted to Instagram, March 5 2024, https://www.instagram.com/reel/C4JZYN6PogS/?utm_source=ig_web_copy_link&igsh=MzRlODBiNWFlZA==.

that your meetings move toward stated objectives. An effective agenda has clearly identified goals. Please note that the agenda is just as helpful in person too. In other words, during our meetings it is not enough to list discussion points. As you prepare your agenda, ask yourself the following:

- What is my desired outcome with this discussion point?
- Is my primary aim providing information?
- Is the team expected to conclude and decide about something by the end of the meeting?
- Should all participants have specific action items after the discussion?

These are valid questions that you should think through as you develop your agenda. Using an agenda during your video conferences allows you time to function with focus. Like in-person meetings, it can be easy to find your team in a set of excessive video conferences with no forward momentum or action.

Set a Consistent Frequency

Finally, as you confer with your team, set consistent meeting times to create habits that allow you to consistently stay connected to your team members. Your regular meetings with team members should include larger team meetings and consistent one-to-one meetings. The frequency of the meetings should impact the duration of your meetings. If you incorporate daily check-ins or huddles with your team, the duration of those meetings does not have to exceed 15 minutes. If meetings are less frequent, you may have longer meetings. However, do not extend meetings unnecessarily. Encourage shorter meetings to ensure your team members are equipped to provide excellent work.

In conclusion, video conferences with your team members can set the tone for how your firm operates and should not be overlooked or neglected. Paying attention to how you create relationships with your staff prepares them to carry out their tasks and unify with your firm's vision. Finally, they'll know what to do during their meetings with the subjects of our next chapter: CLIENTS. But before we turn to the next chapter, let me share some things lawyers can consider regarding video conferencing and recording tools.

Platform Security

Some popular options such as Zoom, Webex, and Microsoft Teams offer end-to-end encryption for meetings. This helps secure the content of the video call while it's in transit. Features such as passwords, waiting rooms, and host controls can help prevent unauthorized access to sensitive material and conversations. Review the platform's security white paper to understand its encryption standards and security measures.

Recording Saving and Storage

Don't rely on cloud storage alone for highly sensitive recordings. Also save them locally to a secure location such as an encrypted external hard drive. Use platform security features like watermarks and screen locks to prevent unauthorized use of recordings. Restrict access and share recordings only with those who should have access. Don't post publicly unless appropriate to do so.

General Recommendations

Discuss confidentiality up front and notify participants if/when recording starts. Reconsider recording where a high level of confidentiality is needed—the safest approach is to not record. Consult information security experts on operational security for handling highly sensitive legal video recordings. The most secure options balance platform security, restrictive access controls, prudent handling processes, and end-to-end encryption when recordings are crucial. But not recording at all is safest for extremely confidential discussions.

6

Video Conferencing with Clients

To maximize connection and trust during a client video conference, one of your primary objectives—especially if this is your first meeting with the client—is to listen. And this is real listening—not the passive type of hearing but actively engaged *listening*.

To the extent that it is possible, you also want to help make it easier for the client or potential client to listen to you. This means that your preparation for the conference should consider how you can eliminate as many distractions as possible for both parties involved. You can do this by investing adequate time in preparing for your consultation, presenting your best self, and having a clear plan for the conference. It is essential to do this because you want to maintain professionalism even in unconventional settings.

LISTENING: A CRITICAL COMPONENT OF TRUST BUILDING

To nurture a sense of trust between you and your existing clients and prospective clients during live video conferences, ensure that opportunities to listen and to be heard are fostered. To assist in this, use appropriate hardware that eliminates technical barriers to transmitting ideas, thoughts, and feelings. We will address these technical components in Chapter 8. For now, as we keep an eye on the big picture and strategy, we will focus on the techniques behind these conversations and then look at ways to implement these strategies through properly aligned tactics.

When it comes to listening, most of us assume that we are excellent listeners because we hear the sounds that others make. Our brains make sense of these sounds and compile them into words, and we form conclusions about what's being communicated. However, the truth is that many of us are poor listeners.[1]

This can be especially true when we are not physically in the same space as someone else, and we are subject to technology that can distract us. I also think those in the legal industry may be even more susceptible to poor listening habits because we have such sharp analytical skills. Because we can quickly take in a lot of information and parse it down to its most essential components, we are often quick to move people toward landing on their points. However, even if you are incredibly skilled at predicting someone's conclusions, which many attorneys believe themselves to be but very few people actually are, listening and creating environments where each party is heard is vital.

Now, your live video conferences may involve different types of meetings. You may find yourself implementing live video for an initial consultation with a lead you hope will eventually become a client. Another live conference may be an instance when you are reviewing an agreement you have crafted for your client. And yet another conference may be an instance in which you are walking your client and team through the execution of an important legal document. There are no cut-and-dried rules that apply to all these various live meetings. However, to pave the way for a focused discussion on the art of listening, it's essential to recognize that certain fundamental principles can significantly enhance the efficacy and efficiency of your live videos.

Effective listening during video conferences can be challenging. This may be due to a wide variety of reasons:

- Perhaps you cannot control your attendees' environment.
- You are attempting to manage the technology of monitoring attendees and ensuring that all the technological components are working the way they should.
- You are also trying to keep track of the information provided to you during the conversation.

[1] Julian Treasure, "5 Ways to Listen Better." *TEDGlobal* 2011, July 2011, video, 7:33, www.ted.com/talks/julian_treasure_5_ways_to_listen_better.

- You may have other applications with notifications running concurrently.
- There are various browser tabs open in the background.

With all these different components vying for your attention, you must be very intentional about staying connected and focused on your video conference. This list doesn't include the natural struggle of switching from one task to another, which, if done abruptly, may not be as effective as one would think. After reading Dr. Cal Newport's work[2] on completing deep work, I wonder if some of our consultations, placed in the middle of our days, are more cognitively akin to interruptions. I imagine the time taken to settle into the conversation and move out of the discussion increases.

I have been guilty of everything I mentioned above, and some of this is inevitable. Still, to the extent possible, as we aim to listen with greater intention, we must try to eliminate those distractions.

First, let's endeavor not to have additional work opened up as we speak with our potential clients. In a virtual environment, the temptation will exist to have various windows and tasks open in the background. During your virtual conferences, minimize these other windows. One reason for doing so is to allow the meeting to be as efficient as possible. If you are distracted during this meeting with your client, you may miss out on crucial information or questions being presented at the time.

Next, if possible, have one person designated as a note taker during the video conference. By assigning the role in advance, you will have increased participation and know that the conversation's ideas and thoughts are effectively captured. So, once again, appoint someone to be your note taker. If you are a solo practitioner and are the only one in your firm, some technological tools can serve as your virtual assistant for note-taking purposes. We delve into that in the following chapter.

WHEN IS VIDEO CONFERENCING APPROPRIATE?

One crucial question to ask yourself as you add video conferencing to your firm's systems is when video conferencing is most effective and appropriate. The right tool applied to the wrong situation transforms that tool into the wrong tool. For the most part, video conferencing is suitable for most client meetings. Even the most strong-willed, extroverted person would concede that a video conference

[2] Cal Newport, *Deep Work: Rules for Focused Success in a Distracted World,* (Grand Central Publishing, 2016).

provides an appropriate environment for introduction and review meetings with clients. The pandemic further confirmed this belief, as it forced practitioners to test whether authentic client connections could occur via video.

Please note that there are some instances when video conferencing may be possible but will have some unique challenges. For example, hosting mediation or negotiations can become complicated without a specified plan of action to improve the process and address logistic issues.

Virtual mediation and negotiations can be challenging due to several logistical obstacles, such as managing documentation, reading body language and visual cues, handling private conversations, fatigue, technical disruptions, and establishing rapport. Document sharing, reviewing, and coediting can be more cumbersome without physical exchange of papers, which can sidetrack discussions.

Reading body language and visual cues is harder to do in video calls, as important nonverbal cues can be missed. Breakout rooms can simulate private sidebar conversations, but virtual environments make it difficult to replicate the ease and secrecy of whispering in someone's ear or passing notes. Fatigue sets in quicker, and negotiation sessions may need to be shorter or more breaks may need to be added to maintain focus.

Technical disruptions, such as internet connectivity issues, device problems, and user difficulties, can temporarily prevent productive talk or derail a planned virtual mediation session. Establishing interpersonal trust and understanding is more difficult virtually than in person due to the barriers and distance that technology imposes between people. Despite these challenges, many mediations and negotiations can still meet their goals through video conferencing, but unique challenges inevitably arise that would not exist when conducted face-to-face. Planning ahead and managing participant expectations around the format are critical for effective sessions.

HOW DOES AN ATTORNEY REVOLUTIONIZE THE WAY THEY INTERACT WITH CLIENTS IN VIDEO CONFERENCES?

To improve how you use your video conferences with your clients, you must ensure that you use video conferences in the most appropriate areas. For example, certain things are best communicated via text or static video. To discover these potential areas where video conferencing may be appropriate, start with the following analytical exercise.

Where Do I Currently Communicate with Clients?

By asking yourself this question, you are starting with a preestablished process. The benefit of starting from this point is the opportunity to do something already somewhat natural to your procedure. A common mistake legal practitioners and laypeople alike make is complicating their natural systems and processes. If your current approach is not detrimental to your goal of engaging with clients, start with where you are.

Ask yourself whether this meeting point or method of communication is sufficient. In other words, does it help my clients? Is it achieving my intended goal? That goal might be to have your clients understand your process or have your clients ready to engage with you if you believe they are a good fit for your firm. Next, ask yourself if this process is efficient. This question speaks to speed and accuracy. Are you able to achieve your goal without a significant loss of time? By asking these questions, you are primed to find areas in your communication with your clients where you can introduce video conferencing.

With these newfound opportunities for connection with your clients, explore how video conferencing can create a unique experience that the client may not be able to have with another firm. In other words, consider gaps within your process that can improve or increase communication. For example, in my business practice, in one season, I provided onboarding meetings with my clients. A client onboarding meeting is designed to welcome new clients into your system and establish the foundations of a healthy attorney–client relationship. Unlike your initial consultation, this meeting is for individuals who have formally engaged your services, and functions as an opportunity to introduce, reinforce, and expand upon your initial interactions. For example, in my work supporting businesses that needed brand protection via trademark registration, the initial 30-minute consultation did not provide sufficient time to diagnosis the client's full trademark leads, qualify the business client, and explain the process in a meaningful manner, so I focused that meeting on the diagnosis and qualification of leads, and left explanations as well as policies and more in-depth procedure walkthroughs to the onboarding meeting.

I found this approach to be extremely valuable for a few reasons:

1. It supported my desire to have a high-touch, concierge law firm.
2. It aligned with other automated processes, and I could explain how we used technology.
3. It gave me a chance to level-set expectations.

4. It provided a chance to preemptively address mistakes I knew clients would likely make based on my experiences with other clients.
5. Finally, it increased communication and decreased the likelihood of grievances before the state bar.

With this established relationship, onboarding focuses more on strategic alignment and optimal use of services rather than assessing fit and qualifications. Onboarding works to integrate a client into established processes and workflows, while an initial consultation evaluates needs to customize an approach.

Increased communication also improves your client's experience. According to the 2021 Clio Legal Trends Report, 67 percent of consumers are interested in working with attorneys who provide remote meeting options in addition to in-person options.[3] By giving these varied connection methods, your client can customize their experience and feel helped. If, as an industry, we fail to adopt our firm practices to reflect what consumers communicate is valuable to help them take care of legal matters, we become impediments instead of advocates.

In addition to the example of providing a cohesive client onboarding experience, consider ways you can provide your essential services via virtual conferencing. For instance, in the estate planning realm, many attorneys now conduct design meetings with their clients to help them create comprehensive estate plans via video conference. Depending on their jurisdictions, many of these same practitioners can conduct execution meetings where all vital documents are signed and notarized via Zoom or another video conferencing platform.

There are several innovative ways to incorporate this technology and improve client relationships when it comes to using video conferences to serve clients. In the next chapter, we will explore how to choose the right video conferencing software for your law firm.

[3] "2021 Legal Trends Report," *Clio*, n.d. www.clio.com/resources/legal-trends/2021-report/. Laura Bagby, "Clio Legal Trends Report Reveals How Clients Want to Communicate with Attorneys," *2Civility*, October 28, 2021, www.2civility.org/clio-legal-trends-report-reveals-how-clients-want-to-communicate-with-attorneys/.

7

Choosing Video Conferencing Software

As you explore ways to incorporate more video conferencing into your practice, you may find that the options for video conference tools abound. After the pandemic, some tools became more popular than others, but do not feel relegated or limited to those options. There are many video conferencing tools available for your various needs.

HOW TO CHOOSE THE BEST TOOL FOR YOU

When exploring the best video conference software—or any tech tool, to be honest—there are several things that you should factor into your decision-making process. The most important factors are the following:

- Purpose
- Budget
- Features/Integrations
- Ease of Use

Purpose

As always, the first question is one of purpose: What will be the primary purpose of my video conferencing software? Will I use this software to talk with my team or clients? What am I hoping to achieve through this interaction? Questions like these may seem simple, but they help frame the rest of your search. If your purpose for video conferencing is not for highly specialized purposes, like sensitive negotiations, specialist consultations, executive interviews, product demonstrations, or virtual summits, that frees you to explore more options and tools. This can be both a positive and negative. It is positive because your needs do not overly constrain you. On the other hand, in some cases, these questions might not do as much to narrow your options. Luckily, there are a few different factors left that may contribute.

Budget

After considering purpose, most individuals consider budget. Your budget should not be the first factor you consider, but it can be considered earlier rather than later. It is essential not to limit your thinking only to what looks like an expense. The better approach is the cost–benefit analysis, where you also consider the return on your investment.

For example, let's look at this analysis through the lens of a legal professional seeking to use video conferencing primarily for the purposes of initial consultations. First, you would want to ask, "What benefits will we gain in the realm of our initial consultations by using this specific tool?" If you are considering Zoom, you may say that the widespread use Zoom aids your primary goal without excessive costs. Alternative video conferencing tools exist, but many of them are for enterprise-level businesses, and their costs and features do not align with your priorities. Some tools may also have equipment costs and transition expenses for training staff and implementing new workflows that should also be considered.

Balancing these factors requires projecting long-term returns, such as expanded client rosters and billable hours, which should offset costs over time. Pricing scenarios should be run to find break-even points based on consultations needed to replace equipment expenses. The analysis should affirm video's value for fueling lasting growth, not just reacting to immediate line items. Implementing the change thoughtfully positions the change to eventually elevate the practice.

Features/Integrations

As we discussed when exploring the various options available, consider what features in your video conferencing tools are essential versus the ones you like and how they fit within the various software.

When evaluating video conferencing platforms, prioritize core functionality for legal consultations over nice-to-have extras. I've provided a breakdown of the most essential versus optional features you can consider:

Essential Features

- **Reliable video quality.** Clear video and audio are vital for remote consultations and presentations.
- **Screen sharing.** The ability to review documents or present slides in real-time is needed.
- **Annotation tools.** Marking up PDFs or adding text to slides helps convey feedback directly.
- **Chat functionality.** The ability to communicate or share information via direct messaging is essential.
- **Recording options.** Clients may want consultations recorded and shared for future review.
- **Security.** Encryption, data protection, and access controls to safeguard client-sensitive information are essential.
- **Simple interfaces.** Minimize hassle in joining calls so users of all tech comfort levels can participate.

The Nice-to-Have Extras

- **Virtual backgrounds.** Visual backdrops help hide messy home offices but aren't essential.
- **Polls/surveys.** Interactive elements are engaging for presentations, less key in one-to-one calls.
- **Virtual breakout rooms.** These are useful for webinars but overkill for typical lawyer–client meetings.
- **Live transcription features.** These are helpful accessibility tools but external services can provide captions alternatively.

The core video, audio, screen sharing, and security foundations enable functional virtual legal consultations. Streamlined interfaces and client control features like recording also facilitate effective sessions. As long as the basics are covered, extras like polls or animated scenes offer supplemental flair but shouldn't drive your decisions in legal contexts focused firmly on functionality.

Ease of Use

Finally, it is essential that whatever software you decide to purchase is user friendly for both you and your intended audience. Choose a platform that is easily accessible if you plan on using it consistently to communicate with clients. This allows you to connect broadly with your potential clients. Consider your comfort level with the tool and how easy it will be for your other video conference participants to utilize it. Key factors influencing usability include intuitive interfaces, flexible options, minimal requirements, strong mobile experience, consistent performance, inclusive features, simple invites, and customer support.

Clean, understandable menus and layouts allow for quick calls and the sharing of screens without complicated settings. Mobile apps should make joining from smartphones seamless. Consistent performance is important too, and inclusive features like closed captioning, phone dial-in numbers, and virtual backgrounds accommodate different needs. Simple invites and customer support, such as troubleshooting guides and webinars, aid in troubleshooting. Prioritizing these factors ensures that you and clients lacking technical confidence can conduct productive virtual consultations. So, pick simplicity, flexibility, and assistance availability for smooth video conferencing experiences.

WHAT ARE THE BEST APPLICATIONS FOR CONDUCTING VIDEO CONFERENCES?

As you explore your video conferencing tool selection, Zoom may be at the top of the list, but several options are available to your firm. We will briefly discuss a few options available as of the writing of this book.

Zoom

No video conferencing list would be complete without mentioning the world's current leader in video conferencing. Aided by the need to find safe alternatives to meeting in person during the pandemic, Zoom emerged as a primary video conferencing software provider. Zoom allows users to partake in video conferencing in a reasonably straightforward manner. A basic in-browser version of Zoom exists, but to fully engage with all of Zoom's most useful and essential features, users are required to download the software. This is one of Zoom's notable drawbacks. However, once the software is downloaded and installed (which is a straightforward process), users can start video conferences with the click of a button. Zoom offers everything from a free version up to more complex webinar subscriptions for larger enterprises.

Zoom's free offering is somewhat limited and would likely not be sufficient for many legal professionals interested in fully integrating video conferencing into their practice. For instance, meeting durations on their free plans are limited to

40 minutes. This limitation alone may pose significant challenges to legal professionals. Additionally, certain integrations with third-party tools are not available unless you are on a paid plan. If you are a legal professional who manages to keep your meetings short and you do not need additional licenses for team members, you may be able to get by with their free plan. Just note that full feature access, including cloud recordings, transcripts, company branding, and admin controls, requires paid plans.

Zoom has grown when it comes to features. When Zoom was on the rise, privacy experts were wary of what seemed to be many privacy vulnerabilities. Issues regarding access to Zoom rooms and encryption shortcomings made some reluctant to rely on Zoom for sensitive matters. This was especially true for attorneys considering how to handle client confidentiality issues and attorney–client privilege. Luckily, Zoom has invested time and money toward addressing those issues.[1] A few improvements in these areas include the following:

- Zoom's ability to automatically implement updates to the software that protects data.
- Increased limitations on who can participate in a Zoom call based on whether they have registered or have been given a unique passcode to enter the room.
- Screen-sharing capabilities are under greater control, allowing the host of a meeting to limit who can share their screens and whether file-sharing capabilities are limited.
- Allowing the host to dismiss and block users or participants who are disruptive.

On the other hand, an upside to the Zoom tool is its many integrations with other SaaS (software as a service) products. Zoom users will find that most scheduling tools like Acuity Scheduling, Calendly, and other digital tools play nicely with Zoom. This means that clients can easily create appointments and, using the integrations available, generate Zoom links that make the virtual rooms where these conferences are held.

---

[1] Andrew Froehlich, West Gate Networks, "How Secure Is Zoom Video Conferencing?," *TechTarget United Communications*, January 19, 2022, www.techtarget.com/searchunifiedcommunications/answer/How-secure-is-Zoom-video-conferencing.

Skype

Another leader in the video conferencing arena is Skype, a long-standing player in video. Unlike Zoom, no download or signup is required to start a video call using Skype. The ease of access and its history as a leader make Skype a valid option for attorneys looking for reliable video conferencing tools. Additionally, Skype is a long-standing solution for placing international calls (and now international video conferences) while avoiding long-distance fees. For many legal professionals, the ability to host Skype-to-phone video conferences gives Skype a significant edge over some of its competitors. Finally, starting a Skype call is simple. After you enter a name for your free call, a unique meeting link will be created for you.

Security is of upmost priority when attorneys evaluate video conferencing tools, especially for sensitive client information. Skype offers an extensive end-to-end encryption to protect call data transmissions, but it has faced security issues in recent years, including lack of built-in password protections, waiting rooms restricting meeting access, and default display of users' IP addresses.

Please note that Microsoft has acquired Skype, so Skype for business is no longer available. You will be asked to upgrade to a Microsoft Teams option if you want more comprehensive features for your video conferences using this platform. That being said, as a Microsoft product, Skype can be a prime target for hackers seeking vulnerabilities, allowing call data access. While Skype facilitates affordable international video connectivity, attorneys dealing with highly confidential client matters should consider supplementary safeguards like disabling IP exposure, requiring passwords, setting up two-factor authentication, and confirming data protections with clients before conducting sensitive consultations. Bolting on extra security precautions helps mitigate Skype's shortcomings compared with platforms like Zoom, which are better equipped to defend against breaches.

Microsoft Teams

If your firm's systems are built around your standard Microsoft suite of tools, you are likely already familiar with our next option, Microsoft Teams. Microsoft Teams in and of itself is a communication system that has a robust video conferencing feature, which does not require the download or registration of an account to access a conference. However, if you want to start a conference, you must log in to your Microsoft account. Another notable feature of the Microsoft Teams option is that participants can access it without downloading the app. You can participate in a Teams video conference using your browser or your phone.

A few other notable features of Teams include the following:

- The ability to share links to your video conference from the conference four different ways: (1) by sharing the link, (2) via your Microsoft Outlook calendar, (3) via your Google calendar, or (4) using your default email.
- The ability to put one video conference on hold while simultaneously participating in another video conference.
- Enhanced formatting options with your chat box allow you to do everything from formatting your text with bold, italic, or strikethrough features to reacting to individual messages from participants.

Teams provides an impressive feature list but does not make it intuitively easy to personalize how you appear to your audience. However, this downside may feel somewhat minimal, given the various enhancements to the video conference options and the fact that it is one part of a comprehensive software suite.

Google Meet

Google Meet is video conferencing software that empowers you to take advantage of the Google ecosystem. Like its counterparts, Google Meet shares similar expected functionalities such as the ability to share your screen, chat with participants, and highlight specific speakers. Some features, however, may require a subscription. For instance, if you would like to record your video conference via Google Meet, you will not be able to do so without enrolling in one of the paid plans available.

On the other hand, one unique feature not often built into its competition is the ability to offer closed captioning for users. Other software typically requires the use of a third-party application.

With Google Meet natively supporting live closed captions without relying on third-party software, it stands out as an accessible choice for attorneys practicing disability law or elder law or who are simply interested in optimizing their firm for accessibility across the board. Autogenerated captions support those with auditory processing issues and allow them to fully participate in virtual consultations.

This helps lawyers better serve clients with diverse physical and cognitive needs. Even attorneys not specializing in accessibility-related practices should ensure their video conferencing tools allow enabling closed captions given many clients across all demographics potentially benefiting from supplementary text displays. Selecting inclusive platforms like Google Meet that build in accessibility instead of adding it as an afterthought demonstrates a broader commitment to serving clients regardless of ability or disability. Given the fact that video calls remove the in-person context clues of body language and facial expressions that aid understanding, offering captions provides vital support—meeting yet another need for tailored communication.

The tools described above are some of the most used as of the time of this writing, but they aren't the only ones on the market—other current options include Webex and GoTo Meeting. And of course, in the future, there may be new players on the scene. As you explore your options, you will discover that there is no one right or wrong answer. As with all typical lawyer responses, the answer to the question of what software I should use is, "It depends." However, use this information to determine the extent to which certain features and benefits matter to you.

8

Level Up Your Video Conferencing

In Chapter 3, we covered the basics of a simple video setup that can be used for video conferencing. There are many instances where this streamlined setup is sufficient. However, you may be interested in elevating your video conferencing presence. Luckily, there are simple strategies available to do this.

When creating a leveled-up video conference experience, here are the most important things to consider:

- How to look better
- How to sound better
- How to improve your hardware and technical connection
- How to enhance the experience

The following sections will unpack the most effective ways to level up in those four areas.

HOW TO LOOK BETTER DURING VIDEO CONFERENCES

Looking your best in any professional setting makes a difference in confidence and earning potential—even on video.[1] Improving the way you look on video

[1] "Best Lighting for Video Conferencing at Home," *HP Official Website*, https://www.hp.com/gb-en/shop/tech-takes/best-lighting-for-video-conferencing-at-home.

conferences does not need to be a dramatic or drastic process. Despite what you may have told yourself in the past, you do not need to have a plastic surgeon reconstruct your face or spend a million dollars with a production company. There are some simple changes you can implement to improve how you look during your next video conference.

The Rule of Thirds

To make your videos more dynamic and engaging consider applying the rule of thirds, a well-known principle in the photography and videography space that involves "creating equally spaced vertical and horizontal lines on a potential shot or image, then placing points of interest on this grid's lines and intersection points. The theory is that the filming style will create more pleasing visuals to the viewer's eye."[2] In other words, when you are recording, think about your scene as if it has been divided into three lines vertically and three lines horizontally. Some cameras (including the ones on most cell phones) allow you to have grid lines to help you with placement. Then use these grids to arrange your primary subjects around this organizational scheme. I use the rule of thirds to make my shots look more dynamic and to ensure that I'm keeping the elements of my video properly focused.

[2] Mina Son, "What Is the Rule of Thirds? Meaning and Examples in Film," *Descript* (blog), September 27, 2023, https://www.descript.com/blog/article/rule-of-thirds#:~:text=The%20rule%20of%20thirds%20involves,visuals%20to%20the%20viewer's%20eye.

ASK TEMI LIVE!!! No
Drama: How to Hire
Members

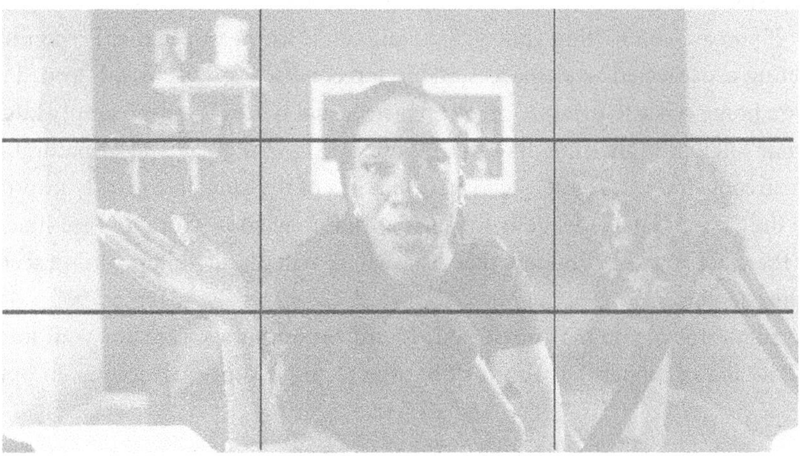

Backgrounds

As discussed earlier, the state of your backdrop can influence your video conferencing experience. To improve the way you appear, you can start by improving your background. You can use your natural background, create a staged area or scene, or utilize a virtual background.

Personally, my preferred method is to use my natural background. Your background may not be one of those perfectly constructed office scenes. However, that adds to the authenticity of the moment. Allow your video conference participants to have a sneak peek into what your world is like. Your office is an ideal space in which to conduct your video conferences.

Is your office more traditional? Does that align with what you want clients and team members to understand about your firm? Or is your firm more modern? If this is the case, use the fact that you will be recording videos as a reason to infuse your personality into the office.

In my office setup, as a black female attorney supporting entrepreneurs, I strategically selected artwork and quotes in my office that would reflect a love of diversity, creativity, and my firm's core mission. The staging of my office communicates just as powerfully in person as it does virtually.

But what if you are working from home?

There is absolutely nothing wrong with conducting video conferences from your home. The pandemic created opportunities for people in all industries to present the realities of their lives without fear. However, a critical consideration if you choose to use the natural background is to be cautious when bringing them into your world: although you are being authentic, it is vital to communicate your professionalism.

If you are conducting your video conference from your home, I recommend creating a dedicated workspace suitable for conducting business. If you do not have a home office to use, one of my favorite visual spaces is a clean empty kitchen. If your kitchen is anything like mine, you may have a great deal of natural light that streams in. As a result, the visual elements of the video are greatly improved. The only potential challenge is the echoes that may come from a space like that, but there are ways to eliminate that risk that we will discuss in upcoming sections of the chapter.

Still, some of you may not be able to utilize common spaces like your kitchen because life is happening. You may be wondering if your bedroom is an option.

I think it is. However, I recommend keeping things like your bed or laundry out of view. I've conducted many video conferences in my bedroom for the past few years. However, during that time, I made it a point to carefully position my camera in a way that nobody was able to guess that I was making my videos from my bedroom. Before finalizing my room setup, I tested various angles and ways I could ensure that the atmosphere created was appropriate for professional video conference calls.

Suppose you are not convinced or would like a more "corporate" or clean feel to your video conference space. In that case, you can also consider investing in an actual backdrop similar to the ones utilized by photographers. These backdrops typically range from $10 to $50 on Amazon. When selecting a backdrop, look for wrinkle-resistant fabrics that can be easily folded and stored when not in use. Solid colors like black, gray, green, or blue look professional and ensure the focus remains on you rather than a busy background. Consider the size of your setup and look for backdrops around 10 feet × 12 feet to easily fill the background behind you. Muslin, microfiber, and canvas materials provide appealing textures at various price points. With the right backdrop, you can create the feel of a dedicated video recording studio right at home.

Now some of you may wonder if a backdrop is okay, then what is wrong with a virtual backdrop? That is an excellent question. Ultimately, having a virtual background is an option, but more often than not, one's virtual background is poorly executed because you may lack the tools to properly create a virtual background that looks good. Failure to execute with a clear virtual background may create the impression that you are not particularly sophisticated.

To level up your use of a virtual background, it is most important to invest in an actual green screen. Seamless virtual backgrounds were made to operate with green screens. There are portable green screens that do not take up too much space. For example, there are circular collapsible green screens that were created to fit on the back of your work chair with a few simple clips.

When looking for a green screen, consider the following factors:

1. **Size.** You need to look for a green screen that's large enough to cover the full area visible with your camera. Common sizes are around 5 feet × 7 feet, but depending on your setup, you may need a larger or smaller one.
2. **Portability.** Look for a green screen that's easy to set up, take down, and move around.

3. **Quality.** Consider high-quality materials that are made of wrinkle-resistant fabrics and are less likely to crease.
4. **Color.** Make sure your green screen provides a green color for effective background removal.
5. **Durability.** Look to customer reviews to evaluate whether the fabric (and the optional accompanying stands) is stable.
6. **Price.** Prices range from $9.99 to $160 on Amazon depending on size and quality.

Without a green screen, you may appear ghost-like on video with strange halos and puzzling ways your body disappears on the camera, so consider purchasing a simple green screen.

Basic green screens can be purchased relatively inexpensively. You may be able to find green screens at

1. **Fabric stores.** You can purchase green fabric by the yard and create your own screen. Muslin or felt works well. Expect to pay $10 to $20 for enough fabric to create a 6 foot × 9 foot backdrop.
2. **Photography stores.** Many photo stores sell portable, foldable green screens intended for photography. A 5 foot × 7 foot screen may cost $30 to $60. Larger 8 foot × 10 foot screens cost around $100.
3. **Amazon.** Tons of budget-friendly green screen options exist on Amazon. A 6 foot × 9 foot screen often costs $30 to $60. Kits with stands and lights typically cost $70 to $150.
4. **General online retailers.** Sites such as eBay, Walmart, and B&H Photo have affordable screens too. Their prices are usually similar to Amazon's.

All in all, you can easily find a solid, basic green screen for less than $100. On the other hand, the more professional-grade, permanent green screens with sturdy stands can run you a few hundred dollars. I'd recommend starting with an inexpensive screen while you're experimenting to see if you even like using a green screen. If you do end up incorporating a virtual background into your video conferencing setup, your investment in using an actual green scene will make your conference setup more refined.

Dress for the Occasion

Another way you can look better is to be intentional about how you prepare yourself. To create compelling videos, you do not need an entire style team. However, as a professional, it is helpful to put some effort into how you are presenting yourself.

For example, we have all seen the video clips of individuals who chose not to wear pants during important conferences because they were home, and at the peak of the pandemic there was no shortage of video clips showing other video conferencing faux pas and Zoom fails. To avoid becoming famous for wardrobe malfunctions, plan what you intend to wear for your video conference, and make sure that your selection is appropriate for the occasion. Please note that this does not necessarily mean that you should wear a full suit. However, avoiding t-shirts and tank tops may be best in this environment to maintain a sense of professionalism.

As to colors, most experts state that bold, bright colors accentuate[3] one's look on Zoom.[4] So feel free to dust off your bold color-block outfits and prints. Be careful with the color white on camera, though. In some instances, it appears beautifully. However, sometimes, a white shirt can project a light that is then enhanced with the lighting you have placed on yourself as a subject. Also, remember not to wear green with a green screen or a virtual background, because it can cause "chroma key" or "green screen spill." This makes your clothing appear transparent or distorted in your final video as the software tries to remove anything green. To prevent this, wear colors that contrast with virtual backgrounds or green screen. Typically, solid colors like blue and gray work well. For those taking it even a step further by applying some form of makeup, ensure that your makeup is not distracting. A common rule for using foundation makeup is to color match your neck. Additionally, consider how various makeup highlights are reflected when light is reflected off it. Poorly blended makeup can create interesting color combinations.[5]

HOW TO IMPROVE THE WAY YOU SOUND

In Chapter 3, we worked on creating a simple setup for sound success. However, there is always room for improvement. If you want to further refine the sound quality of your videos, consider these measures:

1. Adjusting the default settings on your software.
2. Repositioning your microphone.
3. Investing in a higher quality microphone.

---

[3] Rosemary Ravinal, "What You Wear on Zoom Matters. Here's Why," *Rosemary Ravinal: The Master Communicator Blog*, https://rosemaryravinal.com/best-colors-to-wear-video-interview/.

[4] London Image Institute, "How Color Impacts Our Mood," *London Image Institute*, September 10, 2020, https://londonimageinstitute.com/how-color-impacts-our-mood/.

[5] Jenna Rennert, "Follow This 5-Minute Makeup Strategy for Your Next Zoom Meeting," *Vogue*, March 24, 2020, https://www.vogue.com/article/how-to-apply-makeup-for-zoom-video-calls.

Adjusting the Default Settings on Your Software

When we began our video conferencing discussion, we emphasized the need to prepare and have a space conducive to conducting quality video conferences, which remains the same. However, there are simple things you can do to improve your output further. For example, in Zoom, look at the default settings both in the app and via the online system. To access your settings, click on your profile picture or initials in the top right corner of the Zoom window. In the drop-down menu, select "Settings." On your mobile device, tap the "Settings" or "Gear" icon in the Zoom app. The specific settings location may vary slightly based on the device you're using. So, between the settings in these two places, you will discover settings to alter outputs and options to give you greater access to features associated with Zoom, like the use of whiteboards or breakout rooms.

If you've upgraded your microphone, you may have to adjust your software's settings to work with your new microphone. For example, be sure that your software pulls the audio data from the right source, meaning that you want to make sure your computer is properly reading what microphone you are using.

To verify that your software pulls audio data from the correct source (microphone or speaker) during a call, use these steps:

1. Open your video conferencing application on your computer and sign in.
2. Find the settings tab.
3. In the settings, click on the "Audio" tab on the left sidebar.
4. Under the "Microphone" section, you should see a drop-down menu. This allows you to select the microphone source. Ensure the right microphone is selected. You can test it by speaking, and the microphone level indicator should reflect the sound you are making.
5. Verify your speaker settings and ensure the correct speaker is selected. Go ahead and test your audio with the "Test Speaker" and "Test Mic" buttons. This will play a test sound through your selected speaker and allow you to test your microphone.
6. After verifying and adjusting the settings, click the "Apply" or "OK" button to save the changes. Then close the settings window.

Additionally, some microphones may have features that your software may try to add. The effect of this dual feature could reduce the quality of the sound produced. For example, if you are using Zoom and a microphone has echo cancellation, in your settings you'll find a setting entitled "Original sound." You should make sure this setting is on. This will improve the quality of your sound so that the sound is going through two levels of processing.

Readjust Your Microphone

Often, your audience may struggle to hear your sound clearly because you are too close or too far from the microphone, or it is not turned in the right direction. You can use a volume meter, which is necessary for real-time audio feedback. A volume meter is a device that measures the intensity of the sound you produce. If your recording software does not have a volume meter, you can use tools like Audacity, a free audio editor to help you mix and edit your audio tracks.[6]

Monitoring your audio levels gives you optimal recording quality, making Audacity a reliable choice for you regardless of whether you're a beginner or professional in audio editing. Another quick fix to improve your sound is to position your microphone appropriately. This is especially important with microphones that are set to the cardioid pattern. If your microphone is set to this feature, it will collect sound directly in front of it but not from behind it.

If your microphone is on this setting and you have your microphone backward, even if it is on, your microphone will not pick up the sound. On the other hand, if you are too close to your microphone, the position will muffle your sound, and your participants will not make out the words you say. Experiment with various distances to your microphone.

Invest in a Higher Quality Microphone

A third microphone type that we have not yet discussed is the XLR microphone. XLR microphones are the most common type of microphone used at events and on stages. However, they are not commonly used with computers because they do not directly connect to computers and laptops. To use an XLR microphone with your computer, you will first have to connect it to another external device with an audio interface.[7]

Personally, it is not my recommendation that beginners or intermediate users expend money and effort into XLR microphones unless they are ready for all that comes with an XLR setup. Though the gold standard for recording studios, XLRs are more expensive, require the purchase of additional tools, and demand that its users acquire another technical skill. Additionally, the transportation of these tools maybe burdensome.

---

[6] Audacity website, https://www.audacityteam.org/.

[7] J. G. McQuarrie, "USB Microphone vs XLR: Detailed Comparison," *BorisFX|CrumplePop*, November 2, 2022, www.crumplepop.com/usb-mic-vs-xlr/.

Finally, in addition to changing your microphone, consider adding pop filters to your microphones. A pop filter "is a piece of equipment that reduces the popping sounds that occur when you record vocals."[8] They are the puffy covers you typically see on microphones, and they help reduce the intensity of sound that naturally accompanies hard consonants like *p*, *b*, and *t*. In some cases, they are also grid-like mesh filters that do the same job but with a bit more clarity in sound.

In researching these elements, seek out reviews from real users. If possible, find audio tests created by individuals who have these tools. These types of audio tests are often found with a quick YouTube search.

IMPROVE YOUR HARDWARE

Next, consider improving your hardware and its setup. This may mean investing in a new computer or laptop with increased streaming capacity, as evidenced by increased storage. Improving your hardware and optimizing your setup are very important for a seamless video conferencing experience.

1. Testing your internet connection: Before going into hardware upgrades, it's essential to assess your internet connection. Here is a step-by-step guide to help you determine whether your internet speed is sufficient for video conferencing:
    a. *Use online speed testing tools*: Websites like Ookla (Speedtest.net) or Fast.com allow you to quickly check your internet speed and ensure that your upload and download speeds meet the recommended requirements for video conferencing. Ideal speeds for video conferencing can vary, but a stable connection with at least 5 megabits per second (Mbps) for uploads and downloads is generally recommended for high-quality video calls.
    b. *Consider a wired connection*: While Wi-Fi is convenient, a wired (Ethernet) connection often provides more stability and better performance, especially for video conferencing. If possible, connect your computer directly to the router using an Ethernet cable.
    c. *Ground your internet connection*. You can also improve your internet connection. A ground connection will reduce lag time and may aid in your video conference operating without interruption.[9]

[8] MasterClass, "What Does a Pop Filter Do?," September 23, 2021, www.masterclass.com/articles/what-does-a-pop-filter-do/.

[9] "Reduce Lag while Video Live-Streaming," *TechPrate*, December 25, 2020, https://www.techprate.com/digital/reduce-lag-while-video-live-streaming/.

2. Upgrading hardware for video conferencing
   a. *Choosing the right computer or laptop:* Invest in a computer or laptop with sufficient processing power, random-access memory (RAM), and storage. A faster processor and ample RAM can contribute to smoother video streaming and multitasking during conferences. Consider devices with solid-state drives (SSDs) for faster data access, reducing lag and improving overall system responsiveness.
   b. *Selecting quality routers*: The router plays a crucial role in your internet connection. Quality routers from reputable brands like Asus, TP-Link, or Netgear can enhance connectivity and provide advanced features. Look for routers that support the latest Wi-Fi standards (such as Wi-Fi 6) for improved speed and reliability.
   c. *Upgrading network equipment*: If your internet service provider's modem or router is outdated, consider upgrading to newer models. Some ISPs offer modem/router combo devices, but using separate, high-quality devices can provide better performance.
   d. *Consider network boosters or mesh systems*: For larger spaces or areas with Wi-Fi dead zones, consider using network boosters or mesh Wi-Fi systems. These can help extend coverage and maintain a strong connection throughout your home or office.

For more in-depth information on hardware recommendations and networking tips for video conferencing, consider checking reputable technology websites, forums, and guides. Websites like CNET, PCMag, and Tom's Hardware often provide reviews and guides on the latest hardware and networking equipment.

By combining a strong internet connection with quality hardware, you can significantly improve your video conferencing experience, ensuring clear communication and minimizing disruptions during virtual meetings.[10]

HOW TO ENHANCE THE EXPERIENCE

To make sure participants have a positive experience on your video conferences, you should aim to minimize distractions and maximize engagement.

[10] Conor Cawley, "The Best Video Conferencing Equipment in 2024," *Tech.co,* updated January 16, 2024, https://tech.co/web-conferencing/best-video-conferencing-equipment.

Minimizing Distractions

The first thing that may be helpful is to delegate the note-taking. Now, this can be done using technology or it can be done manually. But the main focus is to free participants' minds from thinking about ways to gather every single detail. You can delegate such tasks to an associate, paralegal, or assistant.

If you are the only one running the meeting, you can explore transcription software that securely records and transcribes your video conferences. Tools like otter.ai, Fireflies.ai, and Grain are designed to fit into your company's workflow with integrations with other tools you may be using in your firm. Standard features in these transcription tools include the ability to

- Store recordings
- Identify highlights in conversations
- Search transcripts across conversations
- Segment and share important clips

Please note that while these tools have impressive features that eliminate distractions, they are most effective in situations under a tight schedule. Using these tools on a tight schedule is beneficial because they provide quick transcriptions, aiding in quick information retrieval. Transcribing meetings is helpful for absent participants, helping them stay informed.

Downsides may include occasional inaccuracies in transcription and potential privacy concerns, so weigh the benefits against these considerations. Integrations with other tools streamline workflow, making them suitable for company-wide adoption.[11] These tools will help you keep detailed information and are best used when your agenda effectively provides guidance on the essential items.

One more element to consider is inserting captions into your meeting. Live captions provide opportunities to be more inclusive for your participants and improve communication clarity. Skype, Google Meet, and Microsoft Teams have captioning tools built into the platform. On the other hand, Zoom provides integrations with tools that offer this option. There's an extensive discussion on these platforms in Chapter 7.

Maximizing Engagement

Finally, be intentional about being engaging. This could mean incorporating visual elements and guides in your meeting and switching between showing those

---

[11] Caitlin McMullin, "Transcription and Qualitative Methods: Implications for Third Sector Research." *Voluntas* 34 (2023): 140–53, https://link.springer.com/article/10.1007/s11266-021-00400-3.

graphics and moving back to the participants. You can incorporate polls, Q&A sessions, or breakout discussions; this not only breaks monotony but also actively involves your participants.

Establishing clear objectives is also fundamental for an engaging meeting. By communicating your goals clearly and summarizing key points, your participants stay focused and they understand the purpose of the discussion. Keep meeting times concise, too, avoiding unnecessary tangents and keeping to the agenda.

While there are no guarantees, and technological mishaps occur, with these additional options and strategies for enhancements, you can be sure that your video conferences are leveled up.

PART 3

Video for Marketing

9

Marketing and Branding Primer for Lawyers

"I feel like I already know you."

This was not a random pickup line from someone trying to pique my interest. Instead, this remark came up during an initial consultation with a potential client. This person had viewed some of my educational YouTube videos and decided to explore how I could help them reach their goals. Now, you may be wondering, "What type of content was she creating?" Here's the interesting thing: Most of my videos on YouTube at the time were focused on explaining substantive legal concepts. For the most part, I made very little reference to my personal life. I'm not sure which of the videos they watched or how many they consumed, but the client's trust and excitement were palpable, and I was genuinely surprised. I knew that people found them helpful, but I did not anticipate the bonds that were created. I overlooked one of the most powerful secrets of video: Connection.

Over the years, I have learned that at the heart of impactful video creation lies connection. The legal content I create stands out because it nurtures that sense of connection between the viewer and me, but not in the way one would typically expect. Connection via video creation is not limited to mere entertainment. It is more than making someone laugh or dance. It's showing that you see and understand the viewer and where they are on their journeys through the content you create.

The *Cambridge Dictionary* defines "connection" as "the state of being related to someone or something else."[1] In essence, connections are rooted in relationships. With relationship being the major underpinning for authentic connection, you should be intentional about nurturing connection as you create videos to communicate with potential clients. And this is where marketing and branding meet the world of video.

While ethical fears and concerns were drilled into our minds as law students, the same cannot be said regarding the topics of marketing and branding. Unless one intentionally took business-focused courses or had the unique privilege of having a professor who figured out a way to incorporate this forward-thinking concept into their course, many of you, like me, were not trained in any branding or marketing concepts as attorneys. This lack of discourse regarding this topic can have significant implications.

For example, when I decided to start my practice, I was utterly clueless. I distinctly remember setting up my firm's website and sharing the link with my community on Facebook. I was officially announcing the beginning of my law firm. I was proud of that moment and excitedly waited for the phone to ring.

I waited and waited and waited until it dawned on me that there were probably a few more things I needed to do to connect with clients. As I reflect on those initial months and years, I remember feeling slightly hoodwinked. No one ever warned me that I would have to go and actively find clients. I was under the assumption they would come find me. My urgent drive to find clients led me to explore video marketing, among other strategies. This conversation and primer are birthed from those experiences.

If you are planning on using video as a tactic to find and attract clients, you must have a basic understanding of branding and marketing concepts. And I know that most attorneys would rather not bother themselves with these matters. But for the most part, this topic is relevant to you. Unless you are an employee in a firm with no requirement to help bring in clients, you need to understand and employ marketing and branding strategies to connect with potential leads. This is especially true in these times of "The Great Resignation," the AI revolution, and a season where many law firms are now merging due to problems arising as a result of the pandemic era. Lawyers who still believe they do not have to bring in business may find themselves in a different position at some point in their career.

---

[1] https://dictionary.cambridge.org/us/dictionary/english/connection.

And perhaps you argue that you are not practicing law to make money but to serve. Even if that is the case, you must find the people you are called to serve. Marketing and branding help you do that.

WHAT IS BRANDING?

The most common approach to conversations about marketing starts with proposals regarding tactics, but in most cases, that is putting the cart before the horse. Before you can begin exploring ways to market yourself and your firm using video, you must develop your brand. But what exactly does that mean?

There is no fixed technical meaning of a brand, but there are some general notions that begin to emerge when we explore this idea. The American Marketing Association says that a brand is "a name, term, design, symbol, or any other feature that identifies one seller's good or services as distinct from those of other sellers."[2] On the other hand, Shopify defines branding as "all of the ways you establish an image of your company in your customers' eyes."[3] If branding is defined as that, a brand is the actual image in your client's or audience's heart and mind.

Your brand is about your distinction; for attorneys, this is everything, because ordinary people cannot tell us apart. We all have a list of all the organizations we are part of and have the same standard biography. We list as many fancy badges as possible, but none of these elements distinguishes us to the regular client. What can make the difference, however, is your branding. This is especially true when we have the same four to six marketing companies building the same websites and using the same messages to promote us. When you become intentional about building your brand and connecting with your audience, the clients you can best serve will be attracted to you.

But you must start by identifying your distinction. What critical characteristics in your and your firm's story stand out?

At this point, it is helpful to mention that it is possible and sometimes even advisable to have a firm brand that is distinguishable from your personal brand. Because this book is not a branding book, I will not be able to go into too much

---

[2] Heidi Cohen, "30 Branding Definitions," *Heidi Cohen's Actionable Marketing Guide*, newsletter, August 8, 2011, https://heidicohen.com/30-branding-definitions/.

[3] Daniël Diaz Brea, "The Surprisingly Simple Truth about 'Branding' according to Experts," *Dyseno*, November 11, 2019, https://medium.com/dyseno/the-surprisingly-simple-truth-about-branding-according-to-experts-992cc50f77c4.

depth as to this issue.[4] Additionally, most lawyers reading this book are likely small or solo firm owners, so in these instances, the attorney's brand becomes the firm's brand. The rest of the messaging in this book will lean toward this assumption for ease of consumption.

However, whether we are discussing your personal or business brand, the question is, Who do people say you are? At some point, you must have a clear vision of who you are, and you need to assess whether that vision aligns with the public's perception of who you are. As you read through this section, here are a few questions to help you articulate your brand:[5]

- What are the top five words you would like people to associate with your business?
- What area do you practice in?
- What would you consider to be your core values?
- Why does your work matter to the world?
- What is your big mission?
- What colors and symbols best exemplify your core values?

The idea behind branding is that as you break down these elements, your core market will resonate with those elements. There will be something about you that will be attractive to the clients who are right for you. Then as you continue to engage with this market, you will be able to fine-tune the details that connect with them most. You will gain clarity about the market and be able to speak to them more directly with greater depth. One of my favorite resources for thinking about your market with greater effectiveness is Donald Miller's book, *Building a StoryBrand.*[6]

To make your video marketing efforts consistent with your existing website, you should integrate your video into your current marketing strategy and maintain consistency with your brand identity and website aesthetics. This can be achieved by carrying over visual brand elements from the website to video thumbnails (the placeholder image people see on your video before they click), lower thirds (text or graphics that you show near the bottom lower third of your screen), and ending slides (the last images or graphics shown as your video ends). For example,

[4] Katy M. Goshtasbi, *Personal Branding in One Hour for Lawyers* (American Bar Association, 2013).

[5] Donald Miller, *Building a StoryBrand: Clarify Your Message So Customers Will Listen* (HarperCollins Leadership, 2017).

[6] Ibid.

the videos I create for marketing purposes share the same colors as my overall brand. The videos are part of the entire package. Additionally, when embedding videos into my website, I often customize the playback options to incorporate my overall brand's visuals and messaging. You should be intentional about your call to actions. A call to action is language that directs your viewers as to what they should do next. It could be as simple as "Book now" or "Subscribe."

Consider recording your videos against simple backdrops that echo your website's color palette or use virtual green screens to impose website imagery into the background. Scripted videos should reinforce mission statements and positioning messages from the website while using similar tone/voice. Include links, partner headshots, and service icons on videos that mirror your website styling to strengthen association. Host videos on website pages to directly tie offerings to branded layouts. Tight alignment reinforces marketing resonance rather than diluting it across platforms. With strategic coordination around visual and written branding, video can amplify rather than compete with websites.

In this journey, you will find that video can be instrumental in establishing this brand presence. We will identify the various types of videos you can create and how each can help convey your brand's core element. This is because of the powerful way video shapes perception. Essentially, video is powerful because it allows people to see you. And what they see shapes their understanding of how you can help them solve the problems that matter most to them.

WHAT IS MARKETING?

Now that we have laid a foundation for branding, let us establish a foundation regarding marketing. Branding focuses on your identity and reputation, and marketing is about making you "findable" by the right people. The right people are the folks most likely to need what you are providing and make purchasing decisions. These are the people who have problems that you are qualified to solve. These people are the reason your law firm exists.

Here's the thing. For every 1,000 residents in the United States, there are 4 lawyers.[7] There's an estimated growth of 4 percent for lawyers from now to 2029,[8] so more than enough people need the services that attorneys provide in every

[7] "New ABA Profile of the Legal Profession Report Shines Light on Legal Deserts, High Law School Debt," ABA News Archives, July 22, 2020, https://www.americanbar.org/news/abanews/aba-news-archives/2020/07/new-aba-profile-of-the-legal-profession-report-shines-light-on-l/.

[8] Sharon Miki, "Lawyer Statistics for Success in 2004," *Clio* (blog), December 2020, updated April 15, 2024, https://www.clio.com/blog/lawyer-statistics/.

practice, geographical region, and income bracket. The challenge is that in most instances, these people who need you cannot find you unless you master this essential element of marketing: positioning.

Positioning in marketing means that your brand is visible and findable where your target audience market is located. Essentially, when they need what you offer, they should be able to connect to you quickly. Great marketing and branding make them attracted to you so that you do not have to work as hard to convince them that you are the one to serve them.

The question, though, is, How does this work? Well, it starts by understanding who you are serving with extreme clarity. This is the other part of marketing—discovering your people. Who are the right people most likely to need what you have and buy from you? There are different elements to this question. But these people make up your market. When you have clarity about this group, you have begun to observe patterns about the different things these individuals may have in common. And these observations align with various ways to segment this group from the general population. You can decide to group them based on geography, demographics, psychology, or a combination of all these factors. You may observe certain traits about your market's fears, wants, needs, and interests. To understand this group with this level of depth, you should have a genuine desire to serve them.[9]

Is there a group that you serve or would like to serve? In marketing to them, find out who they are, where they are, and what matters most to them.

Then, take some time to think about your ideal clients. What segments do they belong to? Consider answering the following questions to gain additional clarity about yourself:

- Where are your potential clients located?
- What are they interested in?
- What challenges are they facing?
- What problem(s) do you solve for them?
- How does what you provide save them time, money, or grief?
- What factors influence their decisions?

---

[9] Rebecca Patterson, "Seven Ways to Identify Your Ideal Client," *Forbes*, April 17, 2020, updated December 10, 2021, https://www.forbes.com/sites/forbescoachescouncil/2020/04/17/seven-ways-to-identify-your-ideal-client/?sh=4012a4dc4c21.

These questions go to the heart of finding clarity regarding your target market. When you are clear in these areas, you are equipped to be intentional about how you connect because intentionality is the name of the game.

Expert marketer Donald Miller of the Story Brand framework describes the primary challenge in marketing as noise.[10] Noise, as he describes it, comes from unclear messaging and lacks focus. Without intentionality, attorneys and service providers broadly run the high risk of ineffective tactics that miss the mark. However, when attorneys can home in on their clients' critical priorities and how they uniquely solve those problems, they can then position themselves to communicate these elements more effectively.

KNOW, LIKE, AND TRUST

One element that seems to elude attorneys is how potential clients make decisions. Generally speaking, in our training, we are taught to be outcome oriented. Still, in some jurisdictions, heavy scrutiny is placed on our ability to describe those results from a marketing sense, so we are forced to water down those messages. Additionally, our training teaches us to focus on the soundness of our logic to persuade. Though effective in carrying out our duties as trusted advisors and advocates, these elements are not aligned with how the general public makes buying and hiring decisions.

Regular people hire people they know, like, and trust to solve a problem. These principles, coined by Bob Burg, expert marketer, encapsulate the essential area attorneys must direct their marketing and branding efforts to achieve.[11] In other words, to effectively market you and your practice, you must communicate in a way that allows people to become aware that you exist, meaning you as a person, and believe that you can help them achieve their goals. All three elements are critical, and video is an effective method to meet these objectives.

As we explore video content creation for marketing, we will focus on creating content that

1. Increases awareness regarding your existence and what you do
2. Highlights elements of your personality that your people will love

---

[10] Donald Miller, *Building a StoryBrand: Clarify Your Message So Customers Will Listen* (HarperCollins Leadership, 2017).

[11] Bob Burg, "All Things Being Equal . . . ," *Influence & Impact* (blog), 2010, https://burg.com/2010/04/all-things-being-equal/.

3. Positions you as a trusted authority in your practice area who is well equipped to solve their problems

In addressing those three key objectives, we will try to do so in a way that addresses what I have found to be the most prevalent challenges attorneys face when developing marketing strategies.

First, attorneys struggle to market themselves because of the lack of time. Most attorneys are overworked and underpaid, and the idea of adding a task like "marketing" to the to-do list is daunting. Without a simple systematic way to market that takes less time, attorneys, for the most part, will not market themselves or their practices.

Another challenge some attorneys face is generating the money necessary for marketing efforts. With limited funds, attorneys may find it more challenging to ramp their marketing up and find their way to their audience. With all the various options available to lawyers on how to spend marketing money, this challenge makes the financial burden of marketing as attorneys much more complicated.

Finally, one significant challenge attorneys face in marketing their practices is meeting their leads where they are. Often, attorney marketing fails to truly connect or resonate with the people they are trying to attract. This occurs for several reasons. The first is that attorneys often operate from the faulty assumption that clients know how to distinguish reasonable attorneys from bad attorneys. That distinction is quite challenging in our digital world because of a sense of homogeneousness, particularly in the legal industry.[12]

The tools created to market to leads are often developed by similar companies that fail to highlight the differences that matter most to clients. Additionally, marketing messaging doesn't always properly reflect the levels of skill or success one can anticipate. Instead, most attorneys compete primarily on the number of eyes on their page. Potential clients who visit these pages are often left underwhelmed but are glad they have a starting point in their journey. Attorneys must realize that for their consumers, the difference is often a more robust indicator of who will resonate with a potential client more. One's ability to zero in on distinctions will position attorneys for more success with their target audiences; this is where video comes in. Video creates opportunities for attorneys to use their distinct voices to create distinction and connection with their audience.

---

[12] Jo Hunter, "The 10 Greatest Challenges Facing the Legal Profession in 2022," *Access Legal* (blog), March 25, 2022, https://www.theaccessgroup.com/en-gb/blog/lgl-the-10-greatest-challenges-facing-the-legal-profession-in-2022/.

Marketing Resonance Matrix

During a marketing presentation, I received a question about how to compete in markets flooded with firms that could easily outspend my audience. I wanted to encourage them to lean into their distinctions, leading to increased depth. In trying to come up with the best way to explain the unique challenges and opportunities available to different firms in the marketing world, I created the Marketing Resonance Matrix.

Essentially, when a law firm is involved in marketing, it is possible to have firms that have high marketing and advertising budgets but low impact because they lack depth. On the other hand, smaller firms with smaller budgets may not have the reach desired but may have the significant depth that results in a small selection of raving fans. Then there are the options in between.

Ideally, your firm should work toward the Established quadrant in Figure 9.1. In doing so, your firm will have a broad reach and deep connection.

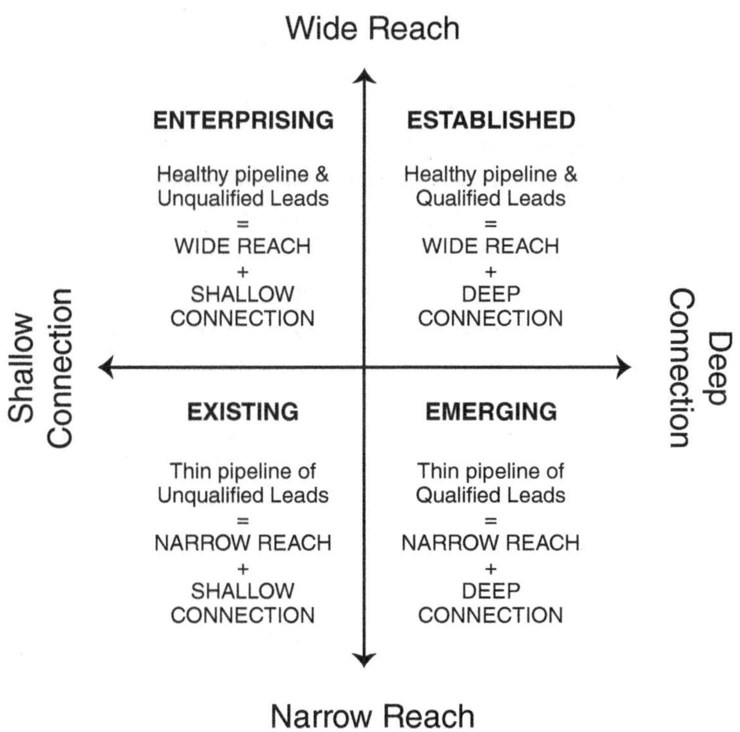

Figure 9.1 The Marketing Resonance Matrix

HOW VIDEO CAN HELP

Video is a powerful tool for marketing your practice. Aside from the numerous statistics proffered by the experts at Wyzowl,[13] the medium creates significant opportunities for both depth of connection and scope of impact. Unlike many other communication methods, video is suitable for repurposing and can therefore allow a creator to expand their reach with a decreased requirement of time. Thus, video is a great way to create omnipresence for firm owners desiring to reach audiences from varying angles.

Here is a list of various methods or channels you can use for videos from a marketing perspective. You can use video in

- Social media marketing
- Search engine optimization marketing
- Email marketing
- Referral-based marketing
- Influencer marketing
- Webinar marketing

Additionally, much of the content created via video can be evergreen because they connect with your audience on a personal level. Infusing information with insightful storytelling will consistently create engagement with your firm.[14] This means that it is not particularly necessary to update certain content aspects frequently. This can be particularly helpful for folks in practice areas that are relatively stable and have limited volatility from a lawmaking perspective.

Now that we have a foundational understanding of key marketing and branding concepts, we will use the following few chapters to explore how to strategize, position, and create marketing videos.

[13] "Video Marketing Statistics 2024," *Wyzowl*, 2024, https://www.wyzowl.com/video-marketing-statistics/.

[14] Digital Marketing Institute, "The Key Role of Video Marketing," *Digital Marketing Institute* (blog), June 19, 2018, https://digitalmarketinginstitute.com/blog/the-importance-of-video-marketing.

10

Planning Video Content for Marketing

The idea of developing a comprehensive video content plan to market your practice can feel overwhelming. You are not alone if you feel plagued by questions like the following:

- What will I say?
- Will anyone care?
- What if this is stupid?
- What if this is wrong?

Because of how overwhelming it can be, I want to start by sharing my process for planning out my videos. Taking the time to develop a clear plan eases the load and improves the overall quality of the videos you create.

To create video marketing content that engages and converts, you must start with understanding your audience. To effectively communicate with any group, you have to know who they are and where they are coming from. In the last chapter, we began exploring concepts related to this, but let's take it a step further here.

GET TO KNOW YOUR AUDIENCE

The longer I'm in business, the more I grow in appreciation for what it means to truly understand your ideal client. When I first began my practice, my understanding was like many attorneys understanding of their clients: Superficial. I had many assumptions about the ways I thought my potential clients navigated the problems I wanted to solve, so I overlooked really connecting with them in a meaningful way. I thought I understood what their priorities were and what their motivations were. But I was often wrong.

For example, I remember a season in my marketing journey were I incorrectly assumed that my clients' most significant challenge in pursuing certain legal services was a lack of knowledge. After many conversations, I eventually found out that was not the case. It was most often a lack of interest in the topic. Clients had a certain dread that they associated with the tasks because (1) they did not think issues would happen to them, and (2) they felt that legal services were merely an expense. With this newfound understanding, I pivoted my content from merely providing information to providing interesting insights about the implications of certain decisions. I wanted them to see themselves in the content I created. So, I shifted my approach based on my market's current point of view.

When creating content to market legal services, you must start where your target audience is—not where you want them to be. Avoid making assumptions about your target market's values. Instead, speak to them and learn who they are. Take the time to engage in active research and social listening as additional strategies to hear your target audience. By understanding your target audience, you empower yourself to create videos that meet their needs and incentivize them to move forward with you.

There are many ways to do this; however, one of my favorite ways to really capture their perspective is by reviewing the questions my clients asked and statements they made before and during our initial consultations. When individuals set up initial consultations with me, they are required to complete an intake form that asks them about why they would like to meet with me. I keep it short, but I always have an open-ended section, and the responses I receive are gold for gaining a better understanding of who they are. Here's why: I periodically review the responses I receive from leads to see if there is a pattern in the way they communicate their problems or the questions they ask. I also use this review to see if there is any information about where they tend to find me. When it came to social media platforms, I became as specific as possible asking, "What platforms and what specific videos?" All this information was then used to refine how I create content, what I say in my content, and where I decide to prioritize placing my content. I also look for patterns during consultations as well.

Along these same lines, when I come across individuals who fit my target demographic, I allow my curiosity to flourish. I ask them questions about the lives they live, the content they consume, their goals, and the things they are focused on. It is amazing what you can learn when you stop making assumptions and start asking questions. I want to encourage you to let your curiosity flourish—even around your referral sources. These individuals engage with your potential clients and have valuable insights that can help you refine your messaging.

As a starting point for you, research your ideal client demographics' social media and viewing habits. Identify relevant LinkedIn groups and Facebook communities your audience actively participates in. This quantifies where people are already investing attention and time. Then match video platforms, lengths, and topics to align with these consumption patterns. For example, different social media platforms have different audiences, and it's important to tailor your content to each platform. Facebook is a great platform for sharing videos that are more personal or emotional in nature, while LinkedIn is better suited for professional content.[1] Also, young entrepreneurs may be more likely than their older counterparts to engage legal guidance through firms found via TikTok or YouTube, favoring concise explainers.[2]

Understanding your audience will then help you evaluate your preferred production style preferences based on your target market. Corporate lawyers seeking corporate clients may expect more polished formal videos aligned to their environments, while families seeking counsel appreciate casual, relatable lawyer interactions on personal channels. The goal is crafting content people immediately recognize as valuable given existing behaviors and needs. Sharing videos organically through communities they already participate in and in formats they instinctively engage amplifies your relevance and shareability.

As you lean into your audience more, you will be able to take the next steps needed in creating your content and generating ideas:

1. *Define your audience and goals.* Who are you trying to reach and what actions do you want them to take after viewing content? Where are they regarding the problems that are most important to them as they relate to what you do? Aligning to specific personas and objectives should inform your later production and distribution choices.
2. *Select the type of video content.* Do you want your videos informational? Do you need testimonials? What about advertisements?

[1] Rochi Zalani, "Posting Like a Pro: What Should You Post on These 8 Social Media Platforms," *Buffer*, September 7, 2017, www.buffer.com/resources/what-to-post-on-each-social-media-platform/.

[2] "Go-To Social Media Video Platforms: Where to Post Your Video Content," *HubSpot* (blog), 2023, https://blog.hubspot.com/marketing/go-to-social-media-video-platforms.

Understanding content genres and their unique value is important as it helps you determine which platform to effectively use and what your video styles would be. This way you don't spend lots of time on the wrong platform.

3. *Choose your video styles and formats.* Will an animation convey your message well? How effective will a talking head video be? Is this content better in long form, short form, or both? Different styles excel for different goals and audiences.

Having a firm strategy for who you want to reach, what overall messages resonate, and what format types accomplish specific aims provides the guardrails for an impactful yet manageable video presence.

Messaging for Multiple Practice Areas

As a quick aside, I did run into a challenge that I want you to be aware of. At the time, I was trying to market to two very distinct practice areas: criminal defense and business law. This created issues in my messaging because it felt inconsistent for my audience for a while. The messaging on defense work did not resonate with my entrepreneurs and the messages on business law did not land well with my target demographic for defense work. I had to really drill down on the two different markets and approach them with even greater scrutiny. Over time, my practice changed so I no longer have those two distinct groups, but I am sure this same issue has come up for someone else.

If you have two or more very different practice areas, developing a clear video marketing strategy will be even more important. Marketing two distinct areas runs the risk of creating conflicting or confusing messaging that fails to engage leads for either of your practice areas. Those who successfully overcome this roadblock do so in the following manner: Some of them have an overarching theme that allows them to make room for both markets. Although they have content that speaks to the individual problems they solve, it's all within a bigger theme. Another way people do this is to develop a separate brand. This gives greater freedom, but it requires more time because you are doing more work. At the end of the day, you can effectively employ distinct video marketing strategies that allow you to connect with your audience without confusing them; however, you have to be intentional in your approach.[3]

[3] "Focused Legal Marketing of Multiple Practice Areas," *FindLaw,* May 22, 2018, www.findlaw.com/legal/practice/law-marketing/focused-legal-marketing-of-multiple-practice-areas.html.

HOW TO CHOOSE A TOPIC

When creating a video, first determine the overall topic you want to address. Consider what issues, questions, or needs your target audience has that your video could help with. Select a topic that you have experience with and can provide value around.

During this stage, keep the situations and experiences of your target audience top of mind. Demonstrate that you understand the problems they are dealing with and have expertise that can guide them. Provide insights around challenges they may be worried about but haven't fully considered yet.

At the same time, be cautious not to cross into offering legal advice. While you likely have experience advising clients in one-to-one conversations, a video reaches a broad audience and requires an appropriate level of care around guidance offered.

As a result, you must carefully craft the topic statement for your video. Please note that in this planning stage, you can still modify it by thinking about what it might be.

If you are struggling to come up with some topics, consider mind mapping. Mind mapping is a free form or stream of consciousness that helps you brainstorm topics on a particular subject. To start a mind map for your video topics, a simple strategy is to start with your subject area, adding branches related to the various types of videos we discussed earlier. Then write out everything you think is related to that topic and that type of video. Cap the amount of time you spend on this activity and be as nonsensical as you want. This is not the time for overcorrection

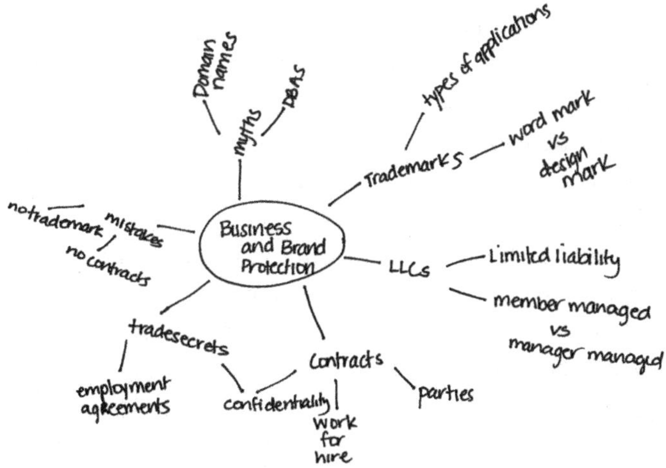

and perfection. Just ideate without judgment. If you find that you are struggling with this practice, there are several online resources to help.[4]

That activity should provide you with a sizable number of ideas. Additionally, a few copywriting tips can make your topics stick. Making a topic "stick" refers to creating topics that resonate memorably, leaving your audience with epiphanies or little aha! moments.[5]

Additional Recommendations for Coming Up with a Topic

1. Make a list of anecdotal experiences you have in your practice area. What topics are these experiences related to? These make good starting points for video topics.
2. Look at popular videos in your niche and think about gaps in the content. Are there subjects or elements of the topic that have not been addressed? Pop culture experiences have many opportunities for legal professionals to fill in gaps because the legal perspective is often missing from the conversation. These gaps can serve as the perfect opportunities to explain how the legal world fits into the broader conversations that are occurring in these spaces.
3. Use the questions clients and leads ask as a starting point. By using actual questions or common misunderstandings, you can rest assured that you are meeting a need.
4. Keep an ongoing list of video ideas as inspiration strikes. Having a running list gives you ideas to pull from later.
5. Ask friends, family, or colleagues what topics they'd be interested in or would want to know more about. This gives insight into likely audience interests.
6. Look for trending topics and news events in your niche area and think about timely videos you could create around them. Being topical can help with views.
7. Don't overthink it initially. You can adjust and pivot over time. Start with something simple that is low pressure and may seem like common knowledge to you. Chances are that someone who is not in the legal profession will find the experience significant.

[4] "How to Mind Map?," *Mindomo*, 2023, https://www.mindomo.com/c/how-to-mind-map/.

[5] Jeffrey Dunn, "What Is 'Sticky Teaching' and How Does It Work?," *Medium*, March 15, 2015, https://medium.com/@jdunns4/what-is-sticky-teaching-and-how-does-it-work-1abe3cc954d8.

After going through these exercises, you should have a sizable amount of topics to choose from. Review your topics and see if they should be broken down into subtopics. If they are better suited as subtopics, you may be able to develop a series or a playlist of videos on this topic to help your audience. This analysis draws attention to an important decision you should make: whether you will create long-form content or short-form content.

When it comes to the distinction between the two, there is no technical term. Some have said that short-form video is video that last less than 3 minutes, whereas before it was content that was less than 10 minutes.[6] In general, I create both, but my priority is creating long-form video and repurposing that content into short-form videos via editing. This is my practice and general recommendation. I believe that longer form content that's created to be evergreen retains its value better than short-form content that is quickly consumed and forgotten. Thought leader Regina Anaejionu has a fascinating thought piece exploring the value propositions offered when it comes to creating content that lasts.[7] So my general recommendation is to make your videos around 10 minutes and repurpose for shorter lengths.

Finally, once you've made your final decision regarding long form versus short form, choose the topic you would like to record your video on. Once that topic is selected, you are ready to move on to outlining.

DEFINE OBJECTIVES

After spending time learning about who my audience was and choosing my topics, I explored where they were in their decision-making process. Taking the time to understand and appreciate a potential client's buying journey should inform the content you create. Over time, as I developed my own process, I began to identify gaps between where I wanted and needed clients to be and where they were when they came across my brand. A few of the gaps, I observed included recognizing that people

- Typically want to keep lawyers away for as long as possible
- Tend to be confused about their rights, how they could enforce them, and who they could turn to for help
- Have different levels of urgency based on how obvious and inevitable the consequences of delay feel for them

---

[6] "Short vs. Long Form Video Content," *Girls in Marketing* (blog), September 21, 2023, https://girlsinmarketing.com/blog/short-vs-long-form-video-content/.

[7] Regina Anaejionu, "Social Media Is All Fun and Games Until Somebody . . . Realizes They're Sharecropping," *byRegina*, November 2021, updated September 2023, https://byregina.com/sharecropping.

Effective legal marketers must be intentional about recognizing that individuals might not be immediately incentivized to take action. Legal work is often viewed as unwanted escalations, expenses, or complications, which makes legal marketing work unique. The marketer's role is to make it easier for those ready to find you and take those steps while simultaneously identifying those who are interested but not yet committed. The same applies to video marketing for a law firm. The goal is typically to build brand awareness, establish expertise, and attract potential clients.

With these new understandings in play, I continued to refine my strategy and define specific objectives to move my client through a process. I decided to work hard on creating content that met people where they were and increased how well they knew me, liked me, and trusted me. Over time, this process became more precise. As a result, I can create video content on various platforms to engage clients, keep my law firm top of mind, and establish myself as a thought leader in my field.

The same can be done for you in your video marketing strategy. As you engage with your ideal client, you should be receiving greater clarity regarding their buyer journey. As you clarify that journey, you will be able to define clear objectives for your video content. This is the next step in your video creation journey.

Taking the time to spell out an objective may seem elementary, but it is critical for success because it helps you create a tightly aligned plan. I learned this secret, as an eighth-grade teacher working through yearly educational goals with my students. Even though we had clearly specified big picture goals as defined by the state, I was charged with determining the learning objectives for my students on a day-to-day basis. Daily objectives were clear statements used to describe precisely what our goal was by the end of a lesson. They would always follow a similar or identical pattern:

OBJ: By the end of today's class, my students will be able to write a cohesive age-appropriate paragraph with a defined main idea.

Similarly, as a legal professional creating video content for your audience, defining your objectives improves the conciseness of your content development process. So, incorporate objectives into your planning process. As you set objectives, consider these pointers:

- Remember who your audience is. As a teacher, my audience was centered on my students. In my practice, my audience is business leaders and decision makers. As attorneys creating videos, we must define our audience. Are you speaking to mothers, entrepreneurs, blue-collar workers, or someone different? Determine this at the onset and allow it to guide you as you craft your objectives.

- Identify the specific type of action you would like your audience to take by the time they are done watching your video. Specifically, determine whether you want them to know something, feel something, or do something. Then explicitly state what that something is. There may be some overlap in these areas as you produce the content, but choosing one as your primary focus is essential.
- Next, identify why achieving this objective is important to your target audience. This step allows you to ensure that what you are doing is relevant or is perceived as applicable to those you intend to connect with.

Let's explore this idea of relevance a bit more.

My favorite high-school teacher was a stickler for ensuring tight organization, and as part of her work in building that skill set in her high school English students, she would have us examine our writing under the *so what test.* I have carried this test and variations of it throughout my professional career and would like to share it with you.

When you are tempted to create a video for your audience, imagine a member of that market asking you, "So what?" Not in a flippant manner but in a way to challenge you to think about why your actions would matter to them. This requires you to step into your audience's shoes and view things from their perspective.

Another benefit of asking, "So what?" is that it keeps you aligned. Ideally, one of your overarching aims should be to help the people you are creating content for. In reviewing things from the perspective of their actual needs, wants, and desires, you can check to see if you are helping them. It eliminates the distraction of doing things just to do them and forces you to focus. The so what test can also help you eliminate excess and clean up what you create.

Writing Out Your Objectives

As you determine your objectives, I recommend that you take a somewhat formulaic approach to writing these objectives out, as in the following templates:

- By the end of this video, [TARGET AUDIENCE] will be able to [SPECIFIC ACTION] so that they can [WHY THIS MATTERS TO THEM].

- By the end of this video, [TARGET AUDIENCE] will feel [SPECIFIC EMOTION] so that they can [WHY THIS MATTERS TO THEM].
- By the end of this video, [TARGET AUDIENCE] will know [SPECIFIC ACTION] so that they can [WHY THIS MATTERS TO THEM].

Here are some examples:

- By the end of this video, emerging entrepreneurs will be able to know the most important factors to consider when choosing an entity so that they can make the entity choices aligned with their long-term goals.
- By the end of this video, recently divorced women with young children will feel inspired and motivated to complete their estate plans so that they won't procrastinate and can have peace of mind that their children are protected.
- By the end of this video, international startups will know the five legal requirements for expanding their businesses into Asian markets so that they can enter new markets and ramp up revenue gains with greater ease.

Let's zero in on the last formula. Consider how we've connected our content to the things that matter most to our audience.

- First, we identify what we want them to do: By the end of this video, individuals accused of crimes will know what to expect at their first court appearance.
- Then we apply the so what test. Why does knowing what to expect at their court appearance matter to your potential client? In this instance, they may be nervous, especially if this is their first time in court. This will help them prepare and alleviate fear. It will also help instill trust in you as their legal counsel.
- When you put it all together you have a clear objective: By the end of this video, individuals facing criminal charges will know what to expect during their first court appearance so that they won't be nervous and do anything that could potentially jeopardize their case.

Intentionally crafting these objective statements at the outset will keep your content relevant to your audience and increase the know, like, and trust factor we discussed earlier. These formulas and tests may seem inconsequential, but they make a difference. These are the same methods I have used and have taught others to use as they develop their law firms' reach using video marketing.

Create a Clear Call to Action

To close the loop on your objective statements, end this portion of your planning by determining what your call to action will be. This call to action should be a natural next step or reflection of achieving the objective you outlined. For example, if your video focuses on immigration matters, your call to action should not be downloading a guide on HIPPA violations. The action should be aligned with the problem or issue you've discussed. One safe call to action to employ is inviting people to schedule a consultation with you.

Essentially, your call to action should be whatever easy step the lead can take if they are interested in further exploring how you can support them. Do not make the mistake of creating highly engaging content and leaving your audience hanging when it comes to what to do next. There should always be a clear, specific call to action to usher viewers to the next stage of the buying process.

To encourage your audience to act, tie your call to action to something that is beneficial to them. If it's a call to subscribe to an email list, try to develop a freebie that they can obtain and here's a hint: it can be a video training, too. If the call to action is something like scheduling a call, provide a special bonus or savings of some sort. Using strategies like this will sweeten the deal for your audience and increase the chances that they will convert from passive observers to active leads.

CHOOSING THE RIGHT VIDEO CONTENT TYPE

Now that you've seen the various video content types there are and how to flesh out that topic, you can now explore and see what type of video best aligns with your objective and audience. In this section, we explore video content types. Saying that you want to create a video without defining what kind of video best meets your needs will leave you frustrated because your video may miss the mark. Let's explore the different types of videos you can incorporate into your marketing strategy. As we explore the different types of videos, you may find yourself discovering other ideas for ways to use these videos outside of your marketing strategy. Please feel free to do this. You are not confined to only using video for conferencing or marketing.

Explainer Videos

Explainer videos are straightforward in that they explain what you do. For legal professionals, an explainer video can present your practice area and why it is essential. Explainer videos communicate complex legal concepts, processes, or services to clients. They can explain the basics of specific areas of law and step-by-step legal processes, and simplify confusing terminology. Explainer videos are very common in the legal industry; however, the most common are filled with legal professionals speaking legalese. They often confuse potential clients and other audience members. They can be extremely effective but must be refined to align with where the audience is in terms of understanding what you are saying. They promote law firms' services, detail working with a firm, and provide overviews of legal rights impacting consumers and small businesses. The goal is to transform dense legal information into engaging, educational content, improving client confidence and transparency, showcasing capabilities, and differentiating firms.

Explainer videos are also excellent places to address the so what issues a client may have, unconsciously or consciously. In some industries, explainer videos may include, in whole or partially, animation. It can be helpful to use animations and drawings to explain more complex concepts, but I strongly recommend using live action to tell the firm's story. The human element is critical for attorneys.

How-Tos

Many people find themselves online looking for guidance on a specific legal task. How-to videos are some of the most popular types of videos you can create to establish yourself as a trustworthy authority on a subject. If your video provides a high-level explanation of how something is done, people will be more inclined to come to you for additional guidance on the topic. One downside, however, to this type of video is that it may also attract many people who are not ready or willing to invest in the next level of work with you. In such instances, the primary value of your how-to value is to expand your brand name and establish yourself as an authority. How-to videos that are most likely to result in more action deal with pressing needs that consumers recognize they cannot address on their own.

Frequently Asked Questions (FAQs)

Are there little annoying questions clients and potential clients ask you repeatedly? Here is the solution:

1. Record a series of short videos answering the questions you never want to explain again.
2. Post them on your website and YouTube channel or platforms where you draw your clients from. It could be TikTok or Instagram for you.
3. When you engage a client or have someone reaching out to you regarding one of these questions, refer them to your list.

Having a list like this allows you to highlight your experience, save time, and exemplify professionalism in one step. Additionally, depending on where you post these answers, you could potentially boost search engine optimization (SEO) results, but there will be more about this in Chapter 12.

Attorneys often believe that the questions must be substantive legal questions. These FAQs can address your most common process questions. These may prove to be more valuable because this is one area that attorneys and legal professionals often overlook. We often forget that most individuals are not as familiar as we are with how things work. Videos addressing questions about how things work in the legal world are valuable to potential clients.

As with your how-to videos, there may be individuals looking for quick answers, but the value in these types of videos cannot be overstated. You can also use this as an opportunity to address your target market's fears that often appear in the form of unanswered questions. In other words, what are the questions your potential client is thinking but is too afraid to ask? If you answer these questions, you will help clients feel relief and trust you.

Testimonials and Case Studies

Videos that feature case studies and testimonials are some of the most powerful videos you can create. They are excellent video sources because they lend themselves easily to one of the most persuasive and engaging methods of connection: storytelling. Even though I have grouped them, there are slight variations between these two types of videos. The primary difference lies in who's telling the story. With testimonials, the story is directly from and directed by the client. These tend to be short and direct and can shed light on the results of working with your firm.

Let your star clients share their enthusiasm about working with you in a video testimonial. Potential clients also value hearing the voices of those who have worked with you. As a result, video testimonials from past clients are golden opportunities to incorporate videos into your firm. These videos are the helpful reviews your potential clients are looking for as they try to choose an attorney.

On the other hand, case studies are more about you as the attorney or your firm and shed light on your process. Extremely effective case studies may feature client testimonials as part of the process. The video experts at Vidyard, a leading video creation company, explain that these videos humanize your business and can lead to increased revenue.[8]

[8] Phoebe Powell, "How to Create Highly Effective Case Study Videos," *Vidyard* (blog), February 19, 2020, https://www.vidyard.com/blog/case-study-videos/.

When creating case study videos, featuring specific client details, we do need to take important ethical precautions around confidentiality and consent. Here are some best practices:

1. Obtain explicit written consent from every client featured in the video to use their case details. Have them approve the specifics of what will be shown.
2. Anonymize identifying client information. Avoid featuring names, images, company identifiers, and the like. Use a voice actor if featuring client audio.
3. Seek guidance from your state bar association/ethics committee about appropriate ways to showcase work without infringing on privilege or confidentiality duties. Protect sensitive case particulars.
4. Frame case studies simplistically rather than highlighting intricate case details. Focus the narrative on broader problems, solutions, and transformations rather than risks, legal arguments, and outcomes.

Answer surface-level questions:

1. What problem did your subject have when they met you? What core problem did the client face?
2. What was the solution you offered the subject to address their pain point? At a high level, what approach/solution did you provide?
3. What result or transformation did the subject experience from working with you? How did this help transform the client's situation?

This technique tells an impactful story while preventing any ethical issues or the accidental disclosure of privileged/confidential case particulars. These three questions follow the common: problem | solution | result format.[9] Within this structure, when preparing these videos, tease each section by exploring the deeper feelings associated with each portion.

For example, as a legal practitioner recording a testimonial, you could ask the subject how they felt about the legal issue. Were they scared, overwhelmed, or annoyed? Have the video capture those emotions. When describing your solution, look at what other solutions your client explored before deciding to engage you. Finally, ask the client how they felt when they experienced the result or relief you promised.

[9] "What is the Difference between Testimonials and Case Studies?" *SuccessKit*, https://successkit.io/what-is-the-difference-between-testimonials-and-case-studies/.

It may also be helpful to consider gathering this data as you serve the client. It may be impractical to expect video documentation throughout the process. Still, you can obtain written feedback from your clients at various stages of the representation so that you will not be starting from scratch when creating your case study video. This may be particularly helpful within our industry because it is not uncommon for legal matters to take some time to resolve.

With testimonials, allow the clients to tell their stories. Use the questions identified above to help your client articulate their experience. As with case studies, when creating these videos, a common concern is confidentiality. To address this, ensure that you are not revealing confidential or incriminating information. Focus more on the real problem, the high-level solution, and the emotions associated throughout. Again, ensure that you have the proper permissions and releases in place.

It's important to note that there are ethics rules governing testimonials and case studies for marketing. These are discussed in detail in Chapter 2 on ethical considerations. It's essential to ensure that you are following ethical best practices when making any type of marketing video, and all the more essential when your videos feature clients.

Myths and Mistakes

There is a unique challenge concerning myths and mistakes videos. Videos that address myths and mistakes are powerful but require careful execution. When done correctly, these videos create powerful aha! moments and leave viewers aware of their need for help. The challenge is that when making these videos, it is easy to overlook gaining the attention of the folks who believe the myth. Essentially, with these videos, the target audience does not realize that they have misunderstood a concept, so legal professionals creating content must lean into exploring ways to capture their audience's attention and disrupt the preliminary views the public may have. One excellent example of a video creator in the legal industry exemplifying this is *LegalEagle*.[10] This YouTube channel, led by attorney Devin Stone, is aimed at uncovering how the law really works and showing its relevance to people in every aspect of their life. One key feature that makes this so effective is Stone's retelling of current events in highly engaging ways. If you are interested in leveraging pop culture into your content, this channel is a fantastic source of inspiration.

[10] Devin Stone, *LegalEagle*, February 1, 2017. YouTube. https://www.youtube.com/c/LegalEagle

Hot Topics and Pop Culture

Speaking of pop culture, timely videos responding to current events or popular culture relevant to your practice area allow you to reaffirm your position and relevance in the mind of your market. These videos are most valuable when the current topics in the news are top of mind, so speed is of the essence. If your production setup is complicated, you may find it challenging to create responses to these events, but don't let that discourage you. Consider using videos like this to pop up on the radar for local news stations seeking to provide unique insights on these topics. Others may request your commentary on such issues if you position yourself as a specialist in certain areas.

After about a year of publishing videos related to popular intellectual property issues in the fashion industry, I was approached by a local reporter to provide legal insights on our local news station. The opportunity produced free publicity and helped to establish me as a thought leader in the field. Attorney Areva Martin also comments on the role of providing relevant and timely commentary when it comes to becoming a rainmaker for your firm.[11]

These videos also provide opportunities to create content that establishes a stance or unique perspective on an issue. Exercise care, however, when taking a view on an issue. Recognize that the internet is not quick to forgive if something is published that is not the best representation of your character. On the other hand, taking a stance on a crucial issue of value to your target client will help you resonate more deeply.

Behind the Scenes

Marketers know this to be true: Your personality is your brand. There is no better way to showcase this personality than sharing day-to-day snapshots. For many of us, recording ourselves daily is daunting and perhaps even off-putting. However, for those with an outgoing, extrovert personality, your potential clients could connect with a video vlog if you feel comfortable sharing. In these instances, clients relate to you personally and trust that you understand their unique plights and are better able to serve those needs.[12] Additionally, you could focus your vlog on the shared interest that unites the community you hope to help.

---

[11] Areva Martin, with Donna Beech, *Make It Rain!: How to Use the Media to Revolutionize Your Business & Brand* (Center Street, 2018).

[12] Court Bishop, "Customer Trust: Why It Matters and How to Build It," *Zendesk* (blog), March 21, 2024, https://www.zendesk.com/blog/customer-trust/.

Behind-the-scenes videos are excellent for increasing your "LIKE" factor. These videos deconstruct the walls of assumptions behind what your work is. In addition to creating a sense of familiarity, use these videos to highlight your process. These videos may present opportunities to explain how things happen in your firm.

Behind-the-scenes videos may also include videos that introduce your team. This can be extremely valuable as you work to empower your team members. Highlighting them in video allows prospective clients to recognize that you do not work in isolation.

Inspirational or Motivational

A final type of video to consider is video that inspires or motivates action. For those of us in the legal profession, we must acknowledge that the natural inclination of the population is not to get lawyers involved unless things have escalated. Nevertheless, inspirational and motivational content can help change that narrative.

Inspirational content shows positive transformation and motivational videos promote taking action rather than the avoidance of most legal action. It helps you incentivize progress and create hope for your target market. For example, this type of inspirational messaging can also resonate with business clients who are looking to turn an idea into reality. A lawyer can assist fledgling entrepreneurs and companies as they bring their visions to life by advising them on legal and regulatory requirements, corporate structuring, intellectual property protections, and crafting contracts and agreements that pave the way for growth. For example, a legal professional hopes to motivate an entrepreneur by depicting the business possibilities available when proactive legal action is taken.

CHOOSING THE RIGHT VIDEO FORMAT TYPE

From the beginning of this book, we have been broadly addressing the video-making process. As we move forward, it is necessary to zoom in on the various types of video formats available to you as you create videos to market you and your firm.

Talking Head Videos

The most common video content you will likely come across or create can be described as a talking head video. This video format involves a speaker looking directly into a camera and speaking to their audience about their chosen subject. We see this form of video daily on the news when a newscaster sits at their desk, looks into the camera, and begins reporting on the news. As an attorney, you can use this exact format to deliver content on a wide variety of content types. This video form does not require a complex setup and can facilitate a meaningful connection between the speaker and their audience. It's useful when trying to connect with audiences on an individual level to teach, persuade, sell, or represent a brand or opinion.

Talking head videos are simple to create and are generally appropriate for all types of content and audiences. The majority of the videos I have created have used this format and they have been very well received because the content is relevant and delivered clearly.

Voice-Over / Screen-Cast Videos

Voice-over and screen-cast videos are another form of communicating certain concepts to your audience. These videos involve video images of your screen with your voice or a narrator's voice speaking about the content being displayed. Sometimes, a video image of the speaker is interposed somewhere on the screen, but the focus remains on the content.

These types of videos are most appropriate when the video's purpose involves displaying some graphics. You may use this format to deliver how-to videos showing clients how to access certain resources, webinars when explaining complex legal concepts you have distilled into simple terms, and behind-the-scenes videos where you are sharing insight regarding your day-to-day routines. You could also use this to show how something works or a process you have developed within your firm.

Animated Video

Another option you can use to incorporate videos into your practice and market is the use of animated videos. These videos usually involve some form of animation used to describe processes or tell the story of a particular subject. As an attorney marketing your practice, an animated video could tell the fictional story of your ideal client and walk them from frustration to solution. This makes animated video the perfect format for explainer videos.

The use of images that simplify and clarify concepts resonate with viewers and help them understand more complex issues that may typically seem overwhelming. Animation is particularly effective for explaining products, services, or abstract concepts to audiences like students, customers, and website visitors. You can also use animated videos to provide how-to videos, myths and mistakes, and some frequently asked questions.

There is information below on the best ways to prepare your outline, but make sure that when it comes to animated videos, you are also considering the visual elements you want to use. It is a very common practice to plan these out scene by scene with story boards. The different scenes should support the main concepts and ideas you are expressing to your audience.

Additionally, unlike other types of video, scripting is absolutely essential. Luckily, the work you have completed so far sets you up for success when it comes to drafting a script. We go into greater detail regarding the pros and cons of scripting later on in this chapter, but here are a few tips to help you successfully script your animated movie:[13]

- Think about your video in sections. These sections can correlate with the different parts of your outline.
- Consider the story behind the problem you are solving or the question you are answering. In other words, what's going on for this person?
- Keep it short. Animated videos do not need to exceed 3 minutes, so your script shouldn't be more than around 450 words.[14]
- Incorporate a clear call to action. An effective animated video will have a next step for a viewer that tells them what action to take and how to take it, so include it in your script.

Interview Mode

Interview videos involve dynamic shots of the subject or multiple subjects engaging in a conversation. When there is only one primary speaker, the video is recorded from various angles, allowing the audience to feel like they are part of an intimate conversation. The interview style may also incorporate elements of the talking head format, depending on the video's purpose. Interview videos are excellent as testimonial videos, which are often focused on telling stories and sharing experiences. This may also be helpful for FAQs videos where two members of the team can discuss the questions and the answers.

---

[13] Animaker Tips, "Explainer Video Script Guide for Beginners," YouTube video, 16:19, uploaded May 17, 2019, https://www.youtube.com/watch?v=SyRqKLtQ71g&t=119s&ab_channel=AnimakerTips.

[14] "How Many Words Should Your Animation Script Be?," *NextDay Animations* (blog), November 5, 2021, https://nextdayanimations.com/how-many-words-should-your-animation-script-be/.

Webinars

Webinars are online educational events created to help teach or reveal something of value to an audience. I compare them with in-person seminars because the objectives between the two are often very similar. With a webinar, presenters provide information to other attendees whose cameras may or may not be on, depending on the host's set up and the participants desires. Information is usually provided from a talking head position with a mix of screen sharing and resource sharing. Webinars can be extremely powerful in turning warm leads into hot converts and creating video clips you can repurpose and share in shorter forms to grow your brand awareness.

Attorneys can effectively use webinars as a marketing tool by hosting introductory webinars to demonstrate their legal expertise and communicate the value they provide. Conducting live Q&A webinars for prospective clients establishes trust and credibility. Interviewing expert guests with relevant insights can attract followers and highlight the host's skills. Pro bono activities can be promoted by inviting nonprofit partners to present related legal topics, demonstrating shared passion for the cause.

During webinars, you can share client success stories as case studies or testimonials to generate confidence about capabilities and outcomes. Enabling webinar attendee questions, promoting across multiple channels, recording content for repurposing, and following up to convert attendees into leads can make authentic relationship building with prospective clients scalable.

This is not an exhaustive list, and with each day, people are discovering new ways to communicate via video. It is not uncommon to see these various types used together to create more dynamic video experiences. As you navigate choosing the format you desire for your videos, do not forget to consider your audience and primary objectives. The format you select should be one that your audience will find engaging while supporting your primary objectives.

OUTLINING YOUR VIDEO

Now that you have selected your format, you are almost ready to record. My recommendation is that you create an outline for your video before you hit "Record." Outlines are very powerful tools for creating cohesive video content that is engaging and meaningful. Because of the nature of outlines, you are forced to think about organization, which will in turn help you present your information in a way your audience will be more readily able to receive.

To start, you write a basic outline including the premise, key points, structure, and any visuals needed. You may want push back and say that you do not typically outline, but I want to encourage you to explore how outlining can help you. As legal professionals, outlines can curtail some of our industry's bad habits (for example, our tendency to overcomplicate things, improperly manage our time, and hoard or gatekeep information) when it comes to communicating.

Using an outline structure can force you to streamline your thoughts in a step-by-step framework. At the end of the day, outlining also improves time management, organization, and the identification of necessary tools you need, allowing for more feasible workloads and meaningful insights delivered in a concise method. When done correctly, your outline will highlight the most critical elements of your video.

As you outline, remember that cohesive content always has a main idea and supporting information. The same concepts should be applied here. Your outline should typically follow this pattern:

1. Attention Grabber
2. Main Objective or Question
3. Application or Supporting Detail 1
4. Application or Supporting Detail 2
5. Application or Supporting Detail . . .
6. Conclusion
7. Call to Action

This outline is applicable to the different types of content you may be considering. Simply modify your outline to fit the format you are using. For example, if you are creating an animated explainer video, you may consider adding specific scenes for each point to help the video remain engaging. If you are hosting a webinar on the most common myths and mistakes in your practice area, your attention grabber could be a startling fact that uncovers the misunderstandings your audience has, and each supporting detail can uncover the implications of the mistaken understanding. The focus is staying aligned with your main objective. All your supporting information should help you encourage your audience to accomplish that stated goal. If you do this, your marketing videos will be clear, relevant, and effective.

THE PROS AND CONS OF SCRIPTS AND TELEPROMPTER OPTIONS

Another aspect regarding recording videos concerns whether you need to prepare a script and read from a teleprompter. That depends on your style. It boils down to personal preference. There are positives and negatives to both options. Some prefer to read from a carefully created script uploaded to a teleprompter. However, many people work from a loose outline. You could also write out a script and memorize it. There are no definitive rules. The goal should be great authentic content that impacts the know, like, and trust factor.

Pros of Scripting

1. Ensures consistent messaging and includes all key details
2. Minimizes "ums," pauses, and so on
3. Allows for careful refining of wording and phrasing
4. Gives predictability for what will be said in the video

Cons of Scripting

1. Can make delivery sound stiff if overrehearsed
2. More challenging to sound natural and conversational

Pros of Speaking Off-the-Cuff

1. Allows for a more casual, impromptu vibe
2. Easy to sound fluid and in-the-moment
3. Ad-libbing generates authenticity and engagement

Cons of Speaking Off-the-Cuff

1. Risks confusing or inconsistent messaging
2. Higher chance for distracting filler words and pauses
3. Content might not be concise or compelling enough

Many creators land somewhere in the middle—using an outline for direction while allowing themselves flexibility in their delivery. My preferred method is the use of an outline. I found that I could decrease prep time and communicate authentically by having an outline. As a result, when recording, I post my outline to a whiteboard in the background or use my iPad for quick referencing. However, I occasionally use a teleprompter with a written script as well. We delve into a bit more detail on selecting a teleprompter in the next chapter that focuses on recording your video.

Regardless of your selected method, the outlines you developed in this chapter should provide a solid foundation for your video. Ultimately, it's about aligning your style, skills, and content goals and trying out what works for you and your audience and sticking with it.

HOW TO COME UP WITH A TITLE

The final part of my video that I work on is its title. I may have a loose working title when the topic is initially selected, but that title is never set in stone because of the dynamic nature of the planning process. By the time, you've spoken to your audience, researched your topic, determined the content, selected a format, and outlined what you'll say, you will be more than ready to tag your video with a title.

As you do this, remember: The title should accurately convey what the content will entail while being compelling enough to generate interest and views. The title should pique viewers' interest and make them want to watch whatever it is that you are creating. One of my favorite types of titles is the direct question because it is typically a question that I have been asked by leads and clients. Next, consider adding a number to the title. Research shows that numbers in marketing content, including video names, result in higher levels of engagement.[15] I'm not sure why this is the case, but I hypothesize that the numbers subconsciously convey a sense of certainty and being less overwhelmed, resulting in audience members feeling more comfortable engaging in the video content you create.[16]

For starters, here is a list of 10 potential titles that can help your topics stand out and help inspire you to develop your first 10 videos:[17]

- The Anatomy of a ___
- 3 Lessons about ____
- ____: An Inside Look at ____
- What You Should Know about ____
- The Truth about ____

[15] J. D. Safran, "Overall Headline Preferences," *Journal of Technical Writing and Communication* 43, no. 4 (2013): 401–13, doi: 10.1177/0047281613493803.

[16] Radostina Iglikova, "The Evolution of the Headline—from Print to Patterns and Virality (an Overview of Research in English and Bulgarian)," *Studies in Linguistics, Culture, and FLT* 4 (2017): 55–69, doi: 10.46687/SILC.2018.v04.005.

[17] Krista Doyle, "How to Title YouTube Videos: 15 Tips (with Real Examples)," *Jasper.ai* (blog), June 4, 2024, https://www.jasper.ai/blog/how-to-title-youtube-videos.

- The Inside Story of ____
- The Consequences of ____
- Want ____? Then Do This
- Why ___ (famous brand or personality) Just _____ (action they took)
- ___ Mistakes That Are Costing You Money

There are also free tech tools that can help you improve your titles and headlines:

- **Portent** (https://www.portent.com/): Portent is a website that offers a free tool for generating creative and engaging titles and headlines. It provides users with suggestions and ideas to enhance the effectiveness of their written content.
- **Orbit Media's Blog** (https://www.orbitmedia.com/blog/writing-headlines/): Orbit Media's blog features a comprehensive guide on writing headlines. The site provides valuable insights, tips, and best practices for creating compelling headlines to capture readers' attention and improve the overall quality of written content.
- **CoSchedule Headline Studio** (https://coschedule.com/headline-studio): CoSchedule's Headline Studio is a free online tool designed to optimize headlines for better performance. It offers analysis and suggestions to help users craft impactful headlines that drive traffic and engagement for their content.

Revisit and refine the title as needed throughout the video creation process. It could be the final thing you do, as developing your topic is more important.

A SUMMARY OF THE STEP-BY-STEP FRAMEWORK

To simplify all the concepts covered in this chapter, here's a step-by-step framework of each step:

1. **Define Your Audience**: Based on the niche you're interested in, describe your target audience. Details like demographics, their likes/dislikes, challenges they face, and questions they have can help guide your content.
2. **Choose Your Topic**: With your audience and practice area in mind, brainstorm a list of 5 to 10 broad video topics that would provide value. These are just general ideas initially. Break your broad topics down into a series of more specific subtopics that each could be the theme of individual videos.

3. **Define Your Objectives**: Look over your broad brainstormed topics and choose one or two that seem most exciting to you and match your audience's needs. Using the "By the end of this video, [TARGET AUDIENCE] will be able to [SPECIFIC ACTION] so that they can [WHY THIS MATTERS TO THEM]" formula creates an objective statement to guide your video creation.
4. **Choose Your Video Content Type**: Now that you have your objective statement, determine what type of content will help you accomplish that objective. If you have multiple options, select the one that your audience would like and that you would enjoy as well.
5. **Choose Your Video Format Type**: Choose the format that would best support your objective, connect with your client, and fit your unique style.
6. **Outline Your Video**: Craft a tight outline to ensure that you stay on topic, relevant, and engaging with your target audience.
7. **Write Out Your Script (Optional)**: Although not required for video production, the use of a script can help ensure that your hard work of research is not wasted. Carefully draft out exactly what you want to say to your audience so that nothing is left out or forgotten.
8. **Determine Your Title**: Select a title that will grab the attention of your target audience and demographic. The title should not be too long and should foreshadow what your video will cover without giving everything away.

Following this framework should take you from a position of not knowing what to talk about all the way through a defined topic and outline for your very first video.

11

Tools for Recording and Editing Your Videos

Whether you're using video for communications, marketing, or both, you should make sure you're using the best tools for the job. This chapter will explore the tools and tech I have used (and some I have not) to make your videos reflect the quality and professionalism you want to achieve.

When it comes to video production, there is a wide range of options available to you. You can produce excellent videos with a very simple setup. You can also choose to explore some subtle details that can continue to level up your video production.

Determining the appropriate setup for your video marketing efforts involves a thoughtful consideration of various factors. First and foremost, clarify your goals—are you aiming for a casual online presence or a more professional and polished image? Next, assess the time you can allocate to video creation; a basic setup may be more suitable if time is limited. Consider the level of support available, whether it's a solo venture or a team effort, as this can influence the complexity of your setup. Budget constraints are also crucial—weigh the costs of equipment, software, and potential outsourcing against your financial resources.

Lastly, evaluate your technological skills; a basic setup might be preferable if you're new to video production, while an enhanced setup may be justified if you possess advanced skills or are willing to invest time in learning. By carefully weighing these factors, you can make an informed decision on the type of video setup that aligns with your specific needs and objectives in video marketing.

RECORDING BASICS

You have all the tools in place. Now it is time to hit "Record." What do you need to do? Do a quick test recording to ensure your frame looks the way you want it to look. Make sure your recording includes sound because you want to check to ensure the sound is connected to the proper recording devices. After your review, you can begin recording. Here is a sample checklist with some suggested items to review before hitting "Record."

I. PREPARE YOURSELF
   A. Gather your notes and or script.
   B. Complete a quick hair and wardrobe check to make sure you look the way you want to look.
   C. Drink water or take a throat lozenge at least 30 minutes before you start recording to prep your body to talk.

II. GATHER YOUR GEAR

   Verify that all your filming gear is ready. Make a checklist of essentials, such as:
   A. Microphones
   B. Camera
   C. Batteries
   D. Spare memory cards

   Go through the checklist to ensure everything is present and functioning properly.

III. ARRANGE YOUR SHOOTING ENVIRONMENT

   Before recording, check your frame composition. Adjust camera angle/framing as needed so the subject is properly framed. Check that lighting is flattering. Adjust room lighting or camera settings as needed. Ensure background is tidy, minimize visual distractions. Basically, follow the checklist here:
   A. Arrange your lighting.
   B. Set up your background.
   C. Set up your tripod.
   D. Adjust any props or visual aids.
   E. Set up your teleprompter.

IV. ADJUST CAMERA SETTINGS
   A. Is the lens clear?
   B. Is it focused appropriately?
   C. Is it zoomed out appropriately?
   D. Is the shot organized around the rule of thirds? (See Chapter 8.)
   E. Set your white balance.
   F. Set your frame rate (30 fps or more).
   G. Adjust the resolution and exposure as necessary.

V. AUDIO CHECKS
   A. Microphone connected?
   B. Levels tested (not too quiet/not too loud)?
   C. External noise minimized?
   D. Video and sound clear?

Now that you have checked everything, it is critical to do a test recording. A test recording confirms that everything is ready to go. All you have to do is record a short clip and confirm if the audio quality, framing, composition, and overall visual and audio quality match up. In addition to test recordings at the beginning of a recording, I often quickly review my recordings throughout the day to ensure that settings haven't changed.

Additionally, listening to your playback will help you develop a vision for the way you want to sound. This may seem elementary, but we often take for granted that we can control certain qualities in our voice. We can be intentional about our speech's dynamics (volume), pitch, and pacing. As you are speaking, you can choose to increase your volume, decrease your speed, and employ varied sounds to emphasize or deemphasize specific points.

For example, in videos where I want to highlight the complexities of a process, I intentionally increase the speed of what I am saying to create a subtle sense of fury. When I want to emphasize the seriousness of a point, I slow down my cadence and sometimes slightly lower my tone. Mastering these elements of speech is not limited to video and enhances the stylistic flair of the videos I produce. This ability to invest in yourself will then ultimately produce higher quality output.

If everything looks good in a test recording, go ahead and hit "Record" to capture the final version. Suppose you are recording a standard talking head video. After you hit the "Start Recording" button, pause for 3 to 5 seconds. You have room to snip some of the extra footage off by taking this time to wait. You may even have room for a transition video at the beginning. Also, pace yourself. Pacing not only helps your potential clients understand your message more clearly, but it also can help you in the editing process.

Regarding editing, what can you do when recording if you make a mistake? Well, pause for about 10 to 20 seconds and see if it is possible to go back to the beginning of the point you are currently explaining. During the editing process, you may find that it will be easier than you think to cut out that portion of your video.

USING A TELEPROMPTER

If you opt to follow a script for your video, you may want to consider investing in a teleprompter. Teleprompters scroll your script as you film for easy readability. Options range from basic DIY setups using tablets to advanced professional grade teleprompters.

When choosing teleprompter styles and software, consider the following factors:

- Your budget constraints
- Desired portability/ease of setup
- Types of content you'll utilize them for
- How tech savvy you are for setup/use
- Entry-level teleprompters like the Glide Gear TMP 100 or Elgato's popular Prompter, which provides lower-cost, basic functionality.
- More sophisticated options like the Autocue prompter offer larger screens, foot controls, and polished setups for frequent filmmakers. Software choices range from free options like Teleprompter to paid tools like the iCue prompter. Reviewing teleprompter recommendations from publications like Videomaker based on your needs is recommended before investing.

If you work with a teleprompter, you can know exactly what to say and consider word choice and language. If you are using a teleprompter, your audience should not be able to tell. In other words, you want to avoid sounding robotic and inauthentic. Mastery of the teleprompter requires practice, and this option will need you to spend time writing out your script. If you prefer this method, there is a broad spectrum of possibilities from a software perspective.

EDITING YOUR VIDEOS

Now that you have created your videos, it is time to edit them and share them with the world. Your editing should make your videos more cohesive, engaging, and impactful. This chapter addresses how to do that.

When it comes to editing simple videos, keep it simple. Avoid attempting to try to do too much as you start. Consider using native editing apps on your phone, computer, or social media apps. For your most basic talking head videos, editing could be as simple as cutting off the first few minutes and last few minutes of the video. If the content is solid and straightforward, that will be sufficient.

Because of the tight process you've employed in your planning, you should find that you have less that needs to be removed. However, do not be scared to eliminate and cut things out. Ruthlessly employ your *so what* test. Please note, though, that the purpose of editing is not to seek or display perfection. Instead, aim to provide authenticity and relevance.

Before we explore these variations, let us spend a few minutes discussing the most common edits and enhancements you can explore. The options are endless, but it is possible to do too much.

Trimming, Splitting, and Merging: The Basics

When it comes to making edits, your basic editing software will have you make the edits on a "timeline." Your timeline is simply "the area of a video editing application where you arrange your video clips and map out all of the edits you would like to apply."[1] Even your social media applications often work with a timeline on the editing side.

One of the most common edits you will likely find yourself making is trimming. Trimming your videos allows you to shorten your video clips by removing excess footage at the end or beginning of a clip. As I mentioned above, for the simplest video edits, this enough. Additionally, almost all, if not all, video editing tools can help you do this. The most typical trim might be cutting off a few seconds from your video that show you moving your hand away from the recorder. You can also cut the last few seconds of you ending your recording.

In addition to trimming, you may find that you want to split certain clips. Splitting lets you divide a long video clip into shorter subclips. You can then delete

[1] Joshua Martin, "An Introduction to the Video Timeline," *Adobe*, n.d., https://www.adobe.com/creativecloud/video/discover/video-timeline.html.

or reorder portions as needed. This is also helpful when starting because you may want to delete portions of the video if you have made a few mistakes. The "razor" or "slice" tool in most editors allows splitting one long clip into shorter subclips. This lets you delete sections or rearrange the order of segments. There may be instances when you record a video, and in retrospect, you realize that you want to change how you ordered the information. Splitting can help you rearrange your clips in your preferred order.

Merging clips takes multiple video clips and combines them into a single clip. This is useful for bringing together different takes or angles into one cohesive sequence. If you are recording multiple takes of a video, you can take the best pieces of the video. Using the merging tools, you can mix clips from different shots when doing a dynamic video. You can combine multiple clips into one video segment using the "Insert" tool or by dragging clips onto each other in the editing timeline. This merges them together. If you are reordering sections of your video, you will probably use merging to reconnect the various parts together in your new preferred order.

Finally, you may want to explore zooming in on portions of your video clips. Using this edit can make your videos look more dynamic and emphasize certain parts of what you say. This effect is closely related to "panning" your video, which may involve zooming in, or moving your focal point from one portion of the clip to another. This movement creates the impression that you were moving your camera while recording. You can use the "scale" and "position" effects to digitally zoom in or pan across a still image. This works by zooming and repositioning the frame over the static photo. You can zoom in or pan into specific details at the various points you want to emphasize in your video.

These video editing affects can also be used to transition between clips. When you have a chance, find a few of your favorite YouTubers, or watch a few scenes in your favorite video. Pay attention to how they transition between clips and scenes. You will notice that they are typically using these basic edits just described. Luckily, you do not need to go to film school to learn how to do the same thing. The various editing tools we will discuss give you the freedom to trim, split, merge, zoom, and so much more.

Adding Captions

Captions are some of the most important edits you can make to your videos today. Captions make your videos more accessible to those who may be hard of hearing.

They also make your videos more engaging for those consuming your content on the go. Suppose you have a potential client considering your firm, and they are watching your video while in public. That environment might not be conducive to turning on the video's sound.

The remarkable thing about this is that many publishing tools can also help you autogenerate these captions. So, once you upload the video on specific platforms, they will detect your words and generate suggested captions. Many of these platforms also allow you to edit the recommended captions just in case they were developed with errors. Some platforms like Zoom, Google Meet, YouTube, discussed in Chapter 7, also produce stylized captions, making your videos more engaging when used appropriately. However, stylized caption or not, whenever possible, incorporate captions into your video.

Images, Graphics, and Text Headings

Another type of edit that you may find helpful concerns graphics and text. I am distinguishing between text and captions because, in these instances, the words are not meant to mark each and everything you say. Instead, you can use text to highlight or summarize critical points you want your audience to remember. How might you use this?

In my videos, one of the things I have tried to implement consistently is short sentences summarizing the key points I'm teaching or presenting to engage my visual learners and pierce through the noise. You can use images and graphics the same way. Are there images that depict your point more clearly? Insert the image into your video. In most of the editing tools, we will look at you can add text with a click of a button. On occasion, however, if I'm use a graphic or something more complex, I might use a tool like Canva (more on this later) to create an image and add it to my editing platform. The platform then usually allows me to add the image to my video clip wherever I want it on the timeline.

Additionally, your more advanced editing tools like Adobe Premiere Pro, Final Cut Pro, or online video editors like Flixier allow you to add text and images to videos using video editing software tools. These tools have templates to easily add titles, labels, introductions, and more. These text overlays can be used for your short sentence summaries or key points. They also allow for inserting images or graphics files directly into the editing timeline, supported in common image formats like JPG, PNG, and SVG. These can be used for diagrams, data visualizations, photos, and other graphics to emphasize points. For example, Adobe Premiere

Pro allows for adding text box overlays, importing images or graphics, resizing and positioning images, and adding fades or transitions between video clips and graphic overlays.

Adding Sounds and Music

Finally, enhance and level up your videos by adding sounds and music. This is not required, but music and sound can communicate emotion to your clients. For example, if you have recorded a talking head video, feel free to add a light audio track in the background. The track should not overshadow or overpower your actual content. For example, consider avoiding tracks with vocals. I personally prefer to use instrumental tracks for that purpose. It should support it, and the theme or tone of the music should align with your overall purpose.

When I'm using music in my videos, I will consider whether my content is happy and energetic and find music to match that tone, or serious and reflective and find more thoughtful music. Again, this is not requirement. It's a nice to have if done well.

You can source royalty-free music from sites like PremiumBeat, Incompetech, and Streamlabs Sound Collection. There are also several subscription sites like Epidemic Sound, Artlist.io, Audioo.com, and Soundstripe.com that provide music with the purchase of a subscription. Once you've found the music you would like to use, most editing software allows easy audio clip integration with footage. Editing tools also have options to fade audio in/out for clean intros/outros. Keep it concise and subtle.

Introductions

You may be considering creating an introduction to your videos. These can be fine, but avoid long, overly stylized introductions. Your viewers are more interested in your information than your introduction. Creating a long, cute intro may be tempting, but that may reduce engagement for those who clicked your video looking for a specific topic.

Copyright and Trademark Considerations

Be sure that if you are using any sounds, music, or graphics, you have a license to use them in the way you've employed them. Ensure that your items fall within that category or that you have paid the appropriate fees to have commercial use of these pieces. There are many royalty-free options for music, images, and video.

TOOLS FOR EDITING VIDEOS

When you are creating videos, it is essential to edit your videos to keep them focused. Here are some popular tools currently used to edit your videos.

Canva

Canva is an online graphic design tool that allows you to create beautiful designs in various formats and forms. One of their more recent enhancements is the ability to edit videos. Using their video editing tool, you can trim video, crop video, and add animations and lovely frames. You can also use Canva to plan your content and share it on various platforms. Additionally, Canva provides team collaboration tools to make receiving and providing feedback easier. Canva has a limited free model, but to have access to their full range of services, the cost currently starts at $14.99 per month. The price is minimal since video editing is only one portion of this dynamic suite.

InShot

Consider using InShot, an all-purpose video editing and video creation app for mobile content. With InShot, you can easily add music, text, and other graphics to create highly engaging videos for prospective clients. InShot can also be used to adjust the speed of your videos, add filters, and make voice-overs simpler. InShot is available via the Google Play app or the Apple App Store. As of this writing, there is a $3.99 monthly subscription, $17.99 yearly subscription option or a $39.99 lifetime fee option.

iMovie and Keynote

Apple's built-in video editing software, iMovie, is built around a video timeline. After importing your video, you can split clips, merge clips, move audio, add music and side effects, add graphics. and incorporate quite a few great features. My first few videos were created using iMovie and Keynote.[2] Keynote is a presentation software similar to PowerPoint for use on Mac devices. Using these tools, I made an introduction video template for my videos. Both iMovie and Keynote come built in for free for Mac users.

---

[2] Kristin Hoppe, "Make Animated Videos with Keynote," *Teachable* (blog), n.d., https://teachable.com/blog/make-animated-videos-keynote.

Clipchamp

An excellent beginner-friendly editing tool is Clipchamp. Clipchamp was acquired by Microsoft in 2021 and has been considered the replacement for Windows Movie Maker. This software is available as a desktop app, an online editor, and a mobile app. It has a suite of intuitive tools features to help you edit your videos. Some of its most notable features include the AI-powered auto captioning, text-to-speech (which allows you to turn text into actual speech in your videos), powerful scene transitions, graphics, and templates. Clipchamp offers only two tiers: a free version and a premium version that unlocks the ability to export videos in 4K and manage your branding within the application. The premium subscription is currently $11.99 per month or $119.99 per year.

CapCut

One of my new favorite editing tools to use is CapCut. CapCut makes somewhat complex editing accessible to the everyday creator. The features are endless. You can do everything from voice changing to transcriptions in other languages to color correction. For individuals easily overwhelmed by too many options, CapCut may seem like a lot to deal with. I recommend CapCut as a stepping-stone between your ultra simple editors like Canva and super complex tools like Final Cut Pro. You can sign up and begin using CapCut's features for free, but to unlock greater storage space consider signing up for the Pro version, currently at $10.99.

Final Cut Pro

This video editing software is also only available for Mac users. Many consider this editor as the more enhanced version of iMovie. It provides more advanced video editing tools and is available for $299.99 from the Apple App Store.

Adobe Premiere Pro and Adobe Premiere Rush

The Adobe Premiere suite of video editing tools provides the full range of video editing tools. Premier Rush is considered the tool for more introductory and beginner video creators who may focus primarily on mobile content. You can shoot, upload, and edit within the app. Premiere Pro provides more professional tools with the ability to add color grading and enhanced audio and sound controls for your video. Experienced and advanced video editors use Premiere Pro to add more enhanced edits. Rush has a free version and one version available for $9.99, whereas Premiere Pro provides a subscription rate as low as $20.99 per month.

Many other editing software and tools are available; however, these are the most common apps you may encounter when searching for video editing tools.

If you need help researching and comparing video production tools and technologies, check out these resources:

1. *The Wirecutter* provides in-depth comparisons and recommendations on cameras, lighting kits, microphones, and editing software
2. *Videomaker* explores beginner, intermediate, and advanced gear picks across all budget levels
3. *TechRadar* profiles the latest video tech releases and ranks products by price and capability
4. *PCMag*'s video section offers buying advice and reviews on video cameras, equipment, and editing tools.

Additionally, there are number of YouTube review videos that highlight many of the most effective and popular options available to you. Here are a few of my favorite YouTube channels for using video:

- Think Media
- Erin on Demand
- Tube Buddy
- Vid IQ

CREATING YOUR THUMBNAIL

Before we end our conversation on editing, let's carefully consider the first image many will see when it comes to your video: your thumbnail. A thumbnail is an image that serves as a placeholder for your video when it is published. It is typically the first thing a potential viewer sees before they decide to click on your video, regardless of whether you are posting on your website, on social media, or on YouTube. It's your video's first impression and it plays an essential role in attracting viewers and encouraging them to click on your content. Consider the following for your thumbnails:

- **Clarity and Relevance**: Your thumbnail should clearly represent the video's content. Avoid misleading viewers with unrelated images. Choose an image that directly relates to the topic of your video. If you're discussing legal matters, consider using legal symbols or relevant visuals.
- **High Contrast and Bold Colors**: Use contrasting colors to make your thumbnail stand out. Bold or cool color combinations according to your brand color can catch the eye. If possible, include a face in your thumbnail. Faces naturally draw attention.

- **Image Quality and Composition**: Use clear, high-resolution images. Blurry or pixelated thumbnails can turn viewers away. Arrange elements (text, images) in a visually pleasing way. Consider the rule of thirds for balanced composition.
- **Text Overlay**: Include a short, descriptive title or key phrase on your thumbnail. When it comes to text on your thumbnail, less is more. Use a font that is easy to read. Aim for something that is readable over something that is beautiful. If possible, you may consider using your brand font or a font that aligns with your overall branding.
- **Proper Dimensions**: Different publishing platforms will display your videos differently and the dimensions for the thumbnail nail image. Adapt your thumbnails for the platform. Canva has an amazing resize tool/feature that helps you replicate your designs in multiple formats with greater ease. For example, thumbnails on YouTube videos should be 1280 × 720 pixels. Ensure your thumbnail looks good on both desktop and mobile devices.
- **Test and Analyze**: Create multiple thumbnail variations and test them with a small audience. See which one performs better. Study successful channels in your niche. What kind of thumbnails do they use? Learn from their strategies. Your thumbnail is like the cover of a book—it should entice viewers to click and explore your content.

I tend to use Canva to develop my thumbnails, but there are various options available. Applications like CapCut have thumbnail tools built in. If you don't manually create a thumbnail, most of your publishing platforms will create one for you automatically. In the next chapter, we will explore the different platforms available to share your videos on and the various features they offer you.

12

Sharing Your Videos

Your video is finished. You hit "Record" and now you are ready to put yourself out there for the world to see. But where should you post your video? Are there some platforms that are better than others? These are some of the questions we will unpack in this chapter. One of the benefits of video is that you can use one piece of content and publish it in multiple places; however, each platform and space has different features that you should consider when prioritizing where to share your content.

YOUR WEBSITE

Your website is one of the most important places to share your videos, but it is often overlooked. Your website is your home online, and video can help make that home more engaging for visitors. Additionally, when effectively employed, video can help make you and your website more findable by search engines via search engine optimization (SEO). According to Vidyard, a leading video messaging platform, "video on websites has the power to increase website traffic, engage visitors, keep people on your site, improve search rankings, [and] bump up conversions."[1]

[1] Kendall Walters, "Video Content 101: How to Use Video on Websites," *Vidyard* (blog), March 15, 2024, https://www.vidyard.com/blog/video-on-websites/.

Most of the videos you create can be published on your website. Some videos that are particularly valuable on your website are the following:

- Introduction videos that share insights regarding the problems you solve
- About Us videos that introduce, you, your team, and your overall purpose and give prospects a chance to connect with you on a more personal level
- Testimonial videos, where clients are describing how you helped them so that you can build trust and credibility
- Explainer videos of Frequently Asked Questions explaining legal concepts, unpacking typical procedures, and addressing client concerns up front

Shared on some of your most frequented pages, these videos will engage your visitors and cause them to stay on your site longer.

There are usually two ways to add videos to your website. One way is to upload the video file directly onto your website. This may be an easier option, but one major drawback is that you are often using up limited server space. The more common alternative to uploading directly onto your website is to host your video on another platform and embed that link into your page.

Although YouTube is sometimes considered a social media platform, it is the world's largest video host and it's free. A few alternatives to YouTube include Vimeo, Wistia, and Dropbox. When you host on another platform, you can usually take a link to the content on the host and paste it into your site. Your website is then able to pull the data from that link and display the video on your webpage.

To further optimize your videos on your websites, do not merely post the video on a page by itself. Always accompany them with relevant text, metadata, and alt text for accessibility. The text on the page should provide context for the video you are sharing. When you do this, you are taking steps that can enhance how well your website performs in search engines like Google.[2] Another alternative is to obtain the transcription of the video and post it as the video's accompanying text on your website. This strategy can positively impact your SEO placement.

Considering this, you could create a video library to add value to your potential clients as they explore your website and evaluate your credibility as a professional. Think strategically about what types of videos to include. Strategically placing a diverse video library on your law firm's website provides an engaging user experience while also opening opportunities for organic discovery. It showcases

[2] Kendall Walters, "Video Content 101: How to Use Video on Websites," *Vidyard* (blog), March 15, 2024, https://www.vidyard.com/blog/video-on-websites/.

your knowledge and compassion for clients in an accessible way while advancing your law SEO efforts.

There are a few other tools that you can use to engage viewers on your website. VideoAsk and Tolstoy are video intake applications that allow you to engage website visitors through video-driven questions. You can use these tools or chatbot options to assess potential client needs and take your potential clients on very targeted journeys. One way to repurpose video using these tools is to use short clips from other pieces of content as video answer responses.

EMAIL MARKETING

Once you've created a new video, consider using video as part of your email marketing strategy. You can take clips of content created for other platforms and share links to these videos within your emails to increase email engagement.

You can also create a lead magnet that incentivizes people to give you their email address in exchange for access to an exclusive email campaign in which you send out a series of videos that help them understand or deal with a specific problem related to your practice area.

To implement this strategy without actually embedding the video into your email, insert an image of the video's thumbnail and hyperlink that thumbnail to the source video for that clip. You can use this strategy to create a video course email sequence.

SOCIAL MEDIA

When it comes to social media and video, its power lies in improving your brand's top-of-mind awareness in your target audience and making you more discoverable by individuals who fit your ideal client profile. Top-of-mind awareness is the idea that when someone is looking for someone in your field, you dominate that space so that you are one of the first, if not the first, brands to come to mind.[3] For attorneys, this means that when someone is looking for someone in your practice area, they think of you first. When that is the case, you have developed solid top-of-mind awareness.

First, social media allows you to provide content curated to communicate a message to your audience. The more you define that message toward a particular group, the more likely you are to resonate with them. Social media also creates

[3] "Top of Mind Awareness: Important Metrics for eCommerce," *ChannelSight* (blog), https://www.channelsight.com/blog/top-of-mind-awareness.

opportunities for individuals who are not yet in the community with you to discover you. Each central platform has features that provide recommendations to its users based on their prior interactions and engagements with their audience. Suppose you can position yourself with discoverable patterns and create content that audiences connect with—which we'll discuss strategies for throughout this section. In that case, these social media platforms will "reward" you by putting you in front of more audience members who enjoyed your content.

Because of how these platforms focus on and promote engaging content, it is also essential to consider whether your target audience or market is on the platform you are considering. Investing time and money could be futile if your target market is not on that platform. Explore each platform to discover if your target audience resides on the platform you are exploring.

Another element of the social media marketing that is important to consider as you explore expanding your use of video on the platforms is the idea that these platforms also allow you to pay to play. This means you can pay for your content to be placed in front of targeted audiences. In other words, you can strategically put your curated content with a clear call to action in front of potential clients.

With these elements at work, social media can help you stand out in your target audience's mind. However, one often overlooked aspect of social media is critical as you develop your marketing plan and determine how you want to share your videos: SEO.

SEO, which stands for search engine optimization, is the idea that you can make yourself, your brand, and your content more discoverable on search engines. Often, however, people approach social media platforms as though they are global search engines. For the most part, they are not.[4] Many of them are evolving to function in that way, but their search engine capabilities are limited to the content on their platforms, whereas platforms like Google search the entire internet for search engines that respond to specific inquiries and search the internet for content that matches these queries. However, much of your social media content is not discoverable via Google's search engine.

The implication for this nuanced distinction is that social media can position you to be the first name a potential client thinks of when they are ready to act and can help you nurture them into a place of action. In contrast, SEO[5] makes you

---

[4] Rochi Zalani, "Getting Spotted on Instagram: How to Ace the Instagram SEO and Get Discovered in Instagram Search," Buffer Marketing Library, August 28, 2023, https://buffer.com/library/instagram-search/#:~:text=What%20is%20Instagram%20Search%2C%20and,re%20searching%20the%20entire%20Internet.

[5] Alexander Hollingsworth, "Guide to Optimizing Video for Search Engines," *Oyova* (blog), April 28, 2023, https://www.com/blog/video-and-seo/.

discoverable for those who are turning to search engines like Google when making those decisions. Recently, more social platforms are making user content findable via search engines like Google and Bing, but how they work vary depending on the platform. This means that what you post as captions, titles, and tags on social media, these can help people who are searching specific topics find you. Understanding this is critical to developing your video placement strategy on social media.

The platforms we will discuss below are primarily social media platforms, but there is one that seems to be both a social media platform and a search engine. As you read through the various platforms, consider what it means to be discoverable on each.

YouTube for Lawyers

Now the first social media platform I'll discuss is my personal favorite when it comes to video marketing: YouTube. One of the primary reasons why YouTube is so valuable is because it is more easily discoverable by global search engines like Google. In other words, your YouTube video is more likely to come up in a Google search than would your Instagram post.

Additionally, users of YouTube tend to go to YouTube in search of something. This means people go to YouTube to actively look for something, whereas on the other platforms, it is more passive consumption. YouTube is the second highest used search engine after Google. And because it is owned by Google, high-performing videos on YouTube are often promoted on Google when individuals search for items.

Consider also that YouTube allows you to host videos. When you create videos and post them to YouTube, many other platforms will enable you to use the YouTube video link and data to share your videos. Finally, if you can create highly engaging content on the platform, you can create an additional revenue source to pay for any ad spend made on the platform. This means that you can earn money for creating YouTube videos. Eligibility for YouTube monetization is limited, though. You must have at least 500 subscribers, 3 public uploads in the past 90 days, and either 3,000 valid public watch hours with long-form videos or 3 million valid public short views.[6]

YouTube provides opportunities to create long-form videos, short-form reel-like videos called YouTube Shorts, live video streams, and video advertising. Each of these video types can create more ways for lawyers to engage clients—long

[6] Lydia Sweatt, "YouTube Relaxes Its Monetization Rules: Only 500 Subscribers Needed!," *VidIQ* (blog), June 13, 2023, https://vidiq.com/blog/post/youtube-relaxes-monetization-rules/.

form for informative deep dives, Shorts for bite-sized content, live streaming for urgency and connection, and video ads to reach motivated audiences seeking legal services. The array of options also allows tailoring your message for different viewer habits and attention spans. YouTube offers far more than just video hosting. Their platform provides attorneys useful features such as the following:

- **Video editor.** Built-in tools to trim/stitch clips
- **Thumbnail creator.** Auto-generate images to showcase videos
- **Chapters.** Break videos into navigable sections
- **Cards/end screens.** Link to websites/other videos
- **Analytics.** Views, traffic sources, audience retention
- **Monetization.** Options to earn ad revenue

Resources to help you utilize YouTube:

- **Creator Academy.** YouTube's official training program. https://www.youtube.com/channel/UCkRfArvrzheW2E7b6SVT7vQ
- **YouTube Help.** Support articles and tutorials found on YouTube. https://support.google.com/youtube/?hl=en#topic=9257498.
- **YouTube blog.** Official news and updates- https://blog.youtube/.

When using YouTube or other platforms to post your videos on Facebook, LinkedIn, or Instagram, as an attorney posting long-form content, here are the keys you need to keep in mind:

- Your Title
- Your Thumbnail
- Your Tags
- Your Description

We will look at each one of these topics in detail. Understanding these elements with YouTube will help you apply these concepts to the following social media platforms. Many of them operate pretty similarly.

- **Your Title.** When selecting a topic for YouTube, remember that people on this platform are often in search of something. To genuinely engage, your content should provide what viewers are looking for. They may be looking for an answer, an experience, a viewpoint, guidance, or insight on that topic. Use the topic list provided in Chapter 10 to create topics that will be "findable" because they will precisely align with what the potential client is looking for.

- **Your Thumbnail.** The thumbnail is an image that serves as the cover of a video or piece of content being shared online. When it comes to YouTube, the thumbnail is what you see when someone scrolls through the list of potential videos to watch. Most platforms automatically generate thumbnails for you. However, you have the opportunity to provide your own custom thumbnails. Take those opportunities. Make your thumbnail inviting so that it stops potential viewers in their tracks. Some strategies for highly engaging thumbnails on any platform are the following:

    1. Use great background pictures. Consider brand photographs that you have as your background photos. With my videos, I often used screenshots from my video clips. Though simple, the pictures produced were high quality.
    2. Crop and adjust the photos to the right to ensure they appear suitable for the platform.
    3. Use text that explains your topic on your thumbnail. The text should not be long, but it should stand out.
    4. Consider using a bright color for your text that contrasts with your background image or laying the words on top of a contrasting block of color. If you are wondering where to create such images, consider looking at Canva, described and discussed in Chapter 11, which has several templates for YouTube thumbnails that you can customize.

With these tips, your videos will stand out, and you will increase the likelihood that they will be clicked when they come up in searches.

Sample Thumbnail

- **Your Tags.** As you upload your video to YouTube, you will discover a section called tags available for you to complete. Do not ignore this area. Tags are where you can include keywords related to the topic of the video. Your keywords should be words associated with how people categorize or describe what they are looking for that you are providing as an answer or response. Keywords are critical to any marketing strategy because they essentially ask you to employ your target audience's language. Fill your keywords to the top. If you are struggling with discovering relevant keywords, there are online tools to help you do keyword research. For example, https://www.wordstream.com/keywords is used to help you identify keywords related to your topic. To see what others in your industry use as a keyword strategy, use a tool like vidIQ or TubeBuddy. This will help you identify successful ways to position your video.
- **Your Description.** Your summary section is also critical. The YouTube algorithm scans the text of your summary for keywords that potential viewers would find valuable. Remember, platforms like YouTube thrive when their audiences are connected with content that meets their needs because it means that the viewer is staying on their platform. You can also consider providing links to references or next steps and a call to action in your summary. As attorneys and legal professionals, summary sections are also excellent places to insert disclaimers reminding viewers that what you provide is for educational and or promotional purposes only.[7] You do not want anyone claiming they became your client by watching a video. If you master the four elements I described and apply them to YouTube and beyond, you will see higher levels of engagement.

To take those strategies to the next level, consider including end screens in your videos. End screens are the popups that appear at the end of your YouTube videos. You can intentionally recommend certain end screens to encourage viewers to consume your content. Similarly, YouTube also allows you to incorporate cards, which are little links to other videos, playlists, or pages of your choice. These

[7] Temitope Siyanbade, "What Is the Difference between a Business and a Brand?," YouTube video, 12:47, uploaded March 26, 2024, https://www.youtube.com/watch?v=fxVx9tp9hp4&t=8s&ab_channel=TemiSiyanbade%2CEsq.%7CBusiness%26BrandStrategist, using the following disclaimer: "Please note that the information I provide on this YouTube channel is for educational purposes only. It does not create an attorney–client relationship. Everyone's situation is different and requires an individualized analysis. Contact a licensed attorney in your jurisdiction if you are facing a legal issue."

can be inserted throughout your video. You may consider using these, if you want to reference other videos you have created.

Finally, consider organizing your content as a playlist. With a playlist, you can curate videos to support your viewers as they look for related information. A well-thought-out playlist can create repeated impressions with a potential lead that boosts your overall engagement. Be sure to promote relevant playlists in the description and comments of your live videos. You can also embed specific videos to autoplay after your live video finishes, directing viewers to more of your content.

After publishing a video on YouTube, visit your analytics page to see

- How many people your video reached
- How long people watched your videos
- Where your audience is located
- How your most recent content compares with older content

Facebook

Facebook is one of the pioneers in social media platforms. Even though it started mainly as a way to connect to friends, Facebook has evolved to be a platform that facilitates connection using multiple means, including video. Like other social media platforms, you can share links to videos on the platform. However, you can also host live video streams through Facebook Live. Data suggests that video engagement on the platform continues to grow.[8]

As you navigate this platform, a few things must be kept in mind. First, the way videos are created and shared between personal pages and video pages will experience differing levels of exposure. Facebook's algorithm results in individual pages receiving more organic visibility than business pages. However, videos uploaded via your business page have more editing and publishing tools available. After publishing a video on a Facebook page, you can see

- How many people your video reached
- How many of those people watched past the first 3 seconds
- The average amount of time someone spent watching your video
- Where your audience is located

---

[8] Jami Oetting, "The Marketer's Guide to Facebook Live [Free Guide]," *HubSpot* (blog), October 6, 2016, updated February 1, 2017, https://blog.hubspot.com/marketing/guide-facebook-live.

Data like this is extremely valuable for understanding your target audience. But please remember that Facebook is not your typical search engine. Your followers may more passively consume your post as you share on your feed and stories. To have your videos reach new potential leads, consider the use of Facebook ads targeted to your specified audience. These Facebook ads allow you to align the group of people you want to see your video.

Instagram

Originally launched in 2010 as a mobile app for sharing photos, Instagram has evolved significantly over the past decade under the guidance of parent company Meta (formerly Facebook). In 2021, Adam Mosseri, the head of Instagram, declared that the platform was "no longer a photo-sharing app or a square photo-sharing app." In a video he posted to the app, he stated that video would be one of the company's primary growth areas. He said, "Video is driving an immense amount of growth online for all the major platforms right now."[9] So the app has focused on experimenting more with video and how to embrace it. As a result, there are many different ways to implement and share your videos with this platform. You can share videos on Instagram as

- **Stories.** A feature that allows users to make various types of content, including video, visible to their followers for up to 24 hours
- **Reels.** Short video clips up to 90 seconds long strung together to convey a story or communicate a thought
- **Posts.** Content shared on the main page of an Instagram user's profile. Reels shared on the account may also remain on their timeline as a post visible to anyone viewing the profile.

Instagram also has opportunities for content creators to run paid advertisements using these various forms of content to generate leads and increase brand visibility.

X (Formerly Twitter)

Although known primarily for short statements (280 characters for free users and most recently 10,000 characters for premium users), Twitter is another platform

[9] Kris Holt, "Instagram Will 'Double Down' on Video in 2022 and Focus on Reels," *Engadget, Oath Tech Network*, December 28, 2021, https://www.engadget.com/instagram-2022-priorities-video-creators-transparency-messaging-adam-mosseri-213020718.html.

where video shared strategically can have a significant impact on improving brand awareness. Data shows that tweets with video attract 10 times more engagement than tweets without video. This means that if you want to stand out on Twitter, video is the way to do that.

Additionally, Twitter provides opportunities to run ads using video. According to Twitter, the most effective Twitter ads have short Twitter copy (use fewer characters), have a clear call to action, and are mobile friendly.

LinkedIn

LinkedIn's focus on professional networking makes it an invaluable platform for lawyers to build connections and promote their services. Legal expertise lends itself well to the referral-based relationships cultivated on LinkedIn. Like other social platforms, LinkedIn now emphasizes video content, providing new opportunities for meaningful video marketing.

An impactful LinkedIn video strategy for attorneys should leverage both video ads and live presentations to highlight thought leadership. Prerecorded video ads allow concise messaging to be sent to targeted demographics. Well-produced legal videos can effectively communicate your practice areas and competitive advantages.

Live video presentations establish subject matter authority by directly showcasing your skills and knowledge. Consider streaming topical legal seminars or workshops to engage your professional community. Interactive broadcasts allow organic relationship building with commenting and questions.

You can also nurture referral relationships by producing serialized video content that offers legal insights for clients and colleagues. For example, provide weekly video summaries unpacking new court rulings and their implications. Or utilize video to weigh in on trending legal issues. Positioning yourself as a trusted source for legal analysis forges productive connections.

There are ample options to integrate video content that reinforces your genuine value, the cornerstone for thriving referral networks. Savvy video marketing campaigns on LinkedIn can significantly expand your visibility and credibility among lucrative professional audiences.

TikTok

TikTok is the viral short-form video platform that has inspired older social media platforms to rethink how short-form video works and how it engages communities.

With the original primary market on TikTok between 17 and 35 years old, the platform was created for lip-syncing and dancing short videos. However, TikTok is increasingly making inroads with older audiences as well. More adults over 35, even into their 50s and beyond, are now using TikTok to connect with younger generations, discover new content, or simply be entertained.

For example, many Baby Boomers and Gen Xers have started using TikTok to create videos showcasing their talents, life experiences, and perspectives for younger viewers. Some find it an engaging way to bond with their grandkids over shared interests and funny videos. Still others like the app's "FYP" page that opens them to an endless stream of novel, amusing content. As TikTok continues to grow, it may soon entirely mainstream itself across all demographics. The platform boasts of over 1 million active monthly users. To maximize the impact of your reach on TikTok, make highly engaging content mirroring the entertainment and education the platform's users are accustomed to. For example, attorney and popular TikTok creator Erika Kullberg creates short tips to help viewers save money by reading the fine print.[10] Her videos are widely shared because she provides short, actionable tips in fun and engaging ways. While some legal professionals have explored TikTok as significant part of their social media strategy, it is important to note that the platform has faced significant legal challenges leaving many wondering whether it will continue to remain in the United States or be heavily regulated.[11]

Now, this is not an all-inclusive list of social media platforms. Snapchat and Pinterest are also powerful platforms that use video. However, I'm not suggesting you need a presence on ALL these sites. Rather, take note of the overarching patterns—platforms aim to keep users engaged with entertaining video that goes viral. Review each site and consider if it aligns with your target demographic and content style. You may find just one or two sites, like YouTube, Facebook, or LinkedIn, that are best suited for your legal practice areas and best resonates with your audience, clients, and legal video content approach. Focus your efforts on those rather than spreading yourself thin trying to post across underperforming platforms.

[10] Erika Kullberg (PR@erika.com), "Money Lawyer Erika on TikTok," https://www.tiktok.com/@erikakullberg?lang=en.

[11] "What a TikTok ban in the US could mean for you," *AP News*, https://apnews.com/article/tiktok-divestment-ban-what-you-need-to-know-5e1ff786e89da10a1b799241ae025406.

REPURPOSING FOR DIFFERENT PLATFORMS

Before we end this chapter, it is also essential to talk about one of the qualities that I believe makes video extremely powerful as a content type, and that is the power of repurposing. Although we've discussed many of these platforms in isolation, there will be many instances where content created for one platform can be reshared or reformatted and shared for another platform. The power in this repurposing ability found with video is that you can be present on multiple platforms in less time.

Podcasts

There are also repurposing opportunities with videos as a podcast. You can extract the audio from the video using the video editors described above. If you are an Apple user, you can also use GarageBand to achieve the same result. Depending on how you've prepared the video, this content can also live online as a video podcast.

When repurposing content for an audio-only format, it's important to consider the visual elements present in the original video. Ensure that the content doesn't heavily rely on visuals, graphics, or on-screen actions that might not translate effectively to an audio-only experience. Narration and verbal explanations should be clear and comprehensive to convey the intended message without visual cues.

Additionally, be mindful of the pacing, as audio content may have different timing requirements than video. Consider the potential loss of engagement that might occur without the visual component and strive to enhance the audio experience with descriptive language and engaging storytelling. Always test the audio version to ensure that it remains compelling and informative, even without the accompanying visuals.

PUBLISHING LIVE VIDEOS

If you are engaging in live streaming, there are a few other strategies and tools to consider. Remember that live streaming on your social media platforms should be part of a cohesive strategy to become top of mind for your clients. Use targeted advertising to position yourself in front of your target audience.

Open Broadcaster Software and Ecamm Live

If you want to enhance the quality of your live streaming by streaming to multiple platforms or adding the editing enhancements like sound, music, and graphics, there are a few options to help. Open Broadcaster Software, also known as OBS, is free software for live streaming and video recording. You can use OBS to stream to YouTube, Facebook, and even your website.[12] You can add audio, graphics, and other elements we have discussed regarding engaging video. OBS has a learning curve, but the powerful and free resources available via OBS may make it more appealing. There is a wide range of tutorial videos available online to guide you. You can screen share presentations or portions of a presentation to create an engaging video.

Ecamm Live[13] is one of my favorite tools. It provides support similar to that of OBS but is created specifically for Macs and has a less steep learning curve. In both tools, you can create graphic overlays during your video. You can easily switch scenes between different cameras or settings for your video. You can even use plug-ins to share live comments on air as your viewers respond to your content. For example, if you are streaming live to YouTube and there are highly engaged individuals chatting live with you, Ecamm has the capability to create a customizable graphic overlay image of the chat message that you can share as part of your broadcast. I like Ecamm Live because it works well with more advanced video setups. Its programming allows it to read data directly from Canon cameras easily, so you can live stream from specific Canon cameras using a USB cord.[14]

Restream

Restream is another online tool that allows you to live stream to multiple platforms easily. Restream can be used with Ecamm live to stream high-quality video on these various platforms. Restream can also utilize its online studio to provide digital overlay frames and other engagement tools. You can also use this tool to bring multiple speakers into your live stream. Restream's online studio provides capabilities like digital overlays, lower thirds, transitions, and more to make your stream highly engaging.

---

[12] "Discover Ecamm Live: All Tutorial Videos," *Ecamm Network, LLC*, n.d., accessed December 4, 2023, https://support.ecamm.com/en/articles/3323109-discover-ecamm-live-all-tutorial-videos.

[13] Jaime Resendiz, "ECAMM LIVE Tutorial for Beginners How to Use ECAMM Live 2023 Step by Step," YouTube video, 16:23, uploaded February 18, 2021, https://www.youtube.com/watch?v=hyCOUpzdbL0.

[14] Alec Johnson, "How to Create Animated Overlays for Ecamm Live (or OBS) Using Keynotes," YouTube video, 15:21, uploaded May 28, 2021, https://www.youtube.com/watch?v=_eIgiCrp4RI.

Additional Considerations for Going "Live"

When going live on platforms like Facebook or YouTube, you don't necessarily have to be filming live in real time. You can record a video ahead of time and then schedule it to premiere as a "live" video at a later date and time. This allows you to fully focus on engaging with and responding to viewer comments during the premiere without having to worry about presenting live on camera.

You can also bring multiple hosts into a live stream using Restream's built-in tools. This allows you to feature special guests for interviews or cohosts for a panel discussion–style live stream. Promote your live streams in advance across your other social media channels to drive more viewers. And be sure later to share recordings of streams as regular videos, too—a single event can provide a lot of repurposable content!

13

Outsourcing Guide

As your video marketing strategy grows, you may find that outsourcing parts of your video creation process is more efficient than becoming an amateur videographer or video editor.

Before you outsource every technical component or portion of the process, establish your goals before you go too far. The goals and objectives you define should drive your search and communication with potential contractors.

ETHICAL CONSIDERATIONS FOR OUTSOURCING VIDEO MARKETING

Before outsourcing your video marketing, remember the ethical requirements of ABA Model Rule 7.2 and Rule 7.3 on responsibilities regarding non-lawyer assistance. We discussed these rules in Chapter 2 and recognized that lawyers have specific rules about how they market their legal services. However, Comment [3] of Rule 7.2 speaks specifically to responsibilities associated with those employed to seek services on behalf of a lawyer.

Suppose an attorney hires staff to assist with marketing efforts. In that case, the attorney must ensure that those conducting marketing activities on their behalf are complying with the appropriate tools and restrictions for attorney marketing. Specifically, Rule 7.2, Comment [3] recognizes that "a lawyer may compensate employees, agents and vendors who are engaged to provide marketing or client development services, such as publicists, public-relations personnel, business-development staff, television and radio station employees or spokespersons and website designers."[1,2]

WHERE CAN YOU FIND CONTRACTORS TO HELP YOU?

Finding help of any kind can be difficult. However, when you know what you are looking for from a contractor, you can better sift through the noise. The best way to find effective help is from word of mouth. However, if you are running into walls, there are common freelancer platforms where individuals can be found. The following are a few platforms:

- Fiverr
- Upwork
- Thumbtack

Once you find someone to help you, it is essential to communicate your vision effectively. For example, depending on their experience level and familiarity with your industry, a video editor may not naturally recognize the vital parts of your video that require emphasis. Feel free to guide what you want for your video(s).

WHAT CAN YOU OUTSOURCE?

For video marketing, there is a broad spectrum of elements that you can outsource. The primary ways I have seen legal professionals and firms implement are discussed in the following sections.

Videography Outsourcing

When outsourcing videography, you're entrusting a professional to capture high-quality footage that aligns with your brand and marketing goals. Consider the following logistical considerations and tips when hiring a videographer:

---

[1] "Model Rules of Professional Conduct—Table of Contents," American Bar Association, n.d., https://www.americanbar.org/groups/professional_responsibility/publications/model_rules_of_professional_conduct/model_rules_of_professional_conduct_table_of_contents/.

[2] William E. Gericke and Thomas G. Wilkinson, "Ethical Implications When Outsourcing Legal Work," *Law Practice Today*, November 13, 2020, https://www.lawpracticetoday.org/article/ethical-implications-when-outsourcing-legal-work/.

Logistical Considerations

1. Portfolio Review: Examine their portfolio to assess the quality and style of their work.
2. Equipment: Ensure the videographer has access to high-quality equipment suitable for your project.
3. Availability: Confirm their availability for the shoot date and any potential revisions.

Tips for Hiring

1. Clear Communication: Ensure the videographer understands your brand, message, and the purpose of the video.
2. Cost Transparency: Clearly outline the budget and discuss any potential additional costs.
3. References: Request references from previous clients to gauge their reliability and professionalism. With this level of outsourcing, you are hiring someone to come in and record your video.

Video Editing Outsourcing

After recording your videos on your own, you can send them to someone to enhance your videos and add some of the creative branding and video elements discussed in this book. Outsourcing video editing allows you to refine your raw footage, adding creative elements and branding. Consider these tips and logistical details when hiring a video editor:

Logistical Considerations

1. Software Proficiency: Confirm their proficiency with video editing software such as Adobe Premiere Pro, Final Cut Pro, or others.
2. Turnaround Time: Discuss the expected turnaround time for the edited video.
3. Revisions: Establish the number of revisions included in the agreement.

Tips for Hiring

1. Editing Style: Ensure the editor's style aligns with your brand and vision for the video.

2. Communication Channels: Set up clear communication channels for feedback and revisions.
3. Rights and Usage: Define the rights and usage permissions for the edited content.

Video Studio Setup Outsourcing

For those who want a system, have the space, and are ready to make video a consistent part of their marketing work, you can hire someone to help you set up your home or office studio. Here are logistical considerations and hiring tips for this:

Logistical Considerations

1. Space Assessment: Assess the available space for the studio setup and equipment.
2. Lighting and Acoustics: Ensure the setup considers proper lighting and acoustics for video production.
3. Equipment Purchase or Rental: Decide whether to purchase or rent the necessary equipment.

Tips for Hiring

1. Experience: Look for professionals with experience in studio setup for video production and with various studio setup styles.
2. Customization: Discuss customization options based on your specific needs and see if they've had this prior experience.
3. Training: Inquire about training or guidance provided for using the setup effectively.

SOCIAL MEDIA MANAGEMENT FOR VIDEO MARKETING

If you need help posting your videos to the relevant platforms, you can find an independent contractor who will help post, promote, or repurpose your videos on these various platforms. Consider these tips and logistical details:

Logistical Considerations

1. Platform Expertise: Ensure the contractor is familiar with the social media platforms relevant to your audience; is it Instagram, YouTube, or TikTok or a mix of them?

2. Posting Schedule: Establish a consistent posting schedule for video content.
3. Analytics Reporting: Discuss the provision of analytics and performance reports.

Tips for Hiring

1. Content Repurposing: Look for contractors who can repurpose video content for different platforms.
2. Engagement Strategy: Look for contractors who can present you with various strategies for engaging with the audience through comments and messages as a starter.
3. Collaboration Tools: Ask contractors about various collaboration tools they've used. And how they can utilize these collaboration tools for seamless communication and content sharing.

YOUTUBE VIDEO STRATEGY AND MANAGEMENT

If you need an overall strategic vision, there are consultants available to help you craft your video marketing strategy, produce high-quality videos, and share them in ways that make a positive difference for your business. Here are logistical details and hiring tips to help you:

Logistical Considerations

1. Content Planning: Ensure they understand how to collaborate on planning a content calendar aligned with your business goals.
2. SEO Optimization: Ensure the consultant understands YouTube SEO for better video visibility.
3. Audience Engagement: Discuss strategies for increasing viewer engagement and subscriber growth.

Tips for Hiring

1. YouTube Algorithm Knowledge: Seek consultants with a deep understanding of YouTube algorithms.
2. Success Metrics: Define key performance indicators (KPIs) and success metrics for the YouTube channel.

3. Collaborative Approach: Look for consultants who value collaboration and are open to refining strategies based on performance data.

By considering these detailed logistical considerations and hiring tips, you can make informed decisions when outsourcing various aspects of your video marketing efforts. Overall, remember that this is part of your firm's marketing strategy. Do not get lost in the details of an area that is not your primary revenue-generating activity. Find your revenue-generating activity, focus on that, and find help to do the rest.

Conclusion

This book is just the beginning of the transformation of how you view your practice and how you connect with clients, team members, and your community. The question for you now is, How far will you take what you've learned? Will you allow it to stay as information tucked away neatly in the back corners of your mind, or will you courageously put yourself out there to see what is possible?

In the Appendix, I've provided resources that I believe will help you apply what you've learned to implement these things into your practice and life immediately. Happy recording!

Appendix 1

Notes for Video Editor

The following note is an email I composed to communicate my vision for my videos with an individual who was helping me edit my videos. By being extremely detailed, I was able to ensure that the person was empowered to execute well.

Hi __________,

I'm excited to work with you on my videos! I've decided to highlight the most important points of each video. Please feel free to use your discretion to modify this list. In other words, these are meant to provide guidance to you without stifling your professional judgment as to how much is too much and the best way to express these points.

Please add my name and necessary information regarding my social media handle, @toslegal.com. As to branding, I don't know if this helps but my website is www.toslegal.com. My social media handle for Twitter, Facebook, and Instagram is @toslegal.

My brand colors are purple, black, white, and gray. The hex code for the purple is #5d2445. My brand fonts are usually Playfair display or Proxima Nova, but I've consistently used Avenir Next Condensed. This is the font I have for my name currently. Let me know if any other information would be helpful.

For the consultation video, please do not use the asked and answer introduction. Use your professional judgment to decide a more appropriate heading.

Do not hesitate to reach out to me with questions and thank you in advance!

Best,
Temi

Appendix 2
Sample Post-Recording Outline

The following outline is an example of guidance I provided to a video editor to help them understand the flow of my videos and the most essential subtopics covered in each video.

1. Before the Consultation
    a. Confirmation Email
    b. Pre-work Questionnaire
2. Preparing for the Consultation
    a. Relevant people
    b. Important documents
    c. Additional notes
3. During the Consultation

What is a sole proprietorship?

1. DBA "Doing business as" a.k.a. Assumed name certificate

Do I need an S corporation?

1. An S corporation is a type of tax election.
2. Requirements:
    a. 100 owners or less
    b. Owners must be U.S. citizens or residents
    c. Only one class of ownership

Acknowledgments

To my father, Emmanuel Tunji Siyanbade, I wish you were here to see this, read this, and watch this all unfold. I remember one of our conversations when I was just getting started with Facebook Live and you told me, "You have to give it a title. What will people call it?" We decided on *ASK TEMI LIVE!* together, and look at where we are now. I love you now and always. Thank you for being my father and teaching me the power of voice. This is only the beginning.

To Mommy, Tunde, and Tomi, I love you all more than words can ever express. I can show up in the world and give love freely because I am so blessed to feel it and receive it from you all every day.

To my amazing tribe of sisters (Stacie, Tochi, Tolu, Tiwa, Ubani, Valentina, and Vivian J.) and my beautiful village of friends who have become family, I am beyond blessed to have you all in my life. I often wonder what I've done to be surrounded by such a dynamic and inspiring group of people. I haven't figured out the answer to that question yet, but I am grateful. Thank you for encouraging me to take up space and share what I have with the world. It has made all the difference.

And finally, thank you to the amazing legal professionals—especially the solo and small law firm owners—who show up and change your worlds every day. Thank you for trusting me. Over the years, you have been my inspiration. Your care for the people and your care for the work move me and inspire me. I honor you and the ways you zealously show up in every facet of our world protecting your clients. The world might not always acknowledge the work you do, but it matters. You are part of a beautiful, noble, evolving world. Don't forget that.

To God, my ultimate source of inspiration, peace, hope, and creativity, thank you.

About the Author

Temi Siyanbade is a speaker and thought leader in the legal tech space. As the principal attorney of her boutique Houston-based law firm and the host of multiple video podcasts, including *The Elevated Esquire* and *ASK TEMI LIVE!*, her services focus on strategically positioning businesses for long-term success, meaningful impact, and innovative business development.

Temi has had the privilege of speaking to diverse audiences and industries, including the American Bar Association and the National Business Institute. With compelling stories that shift mindsets and eye-opening information that alters outlooks, Temi provides a different approach to transformation activation in her audiences.

Having taught middle school English as a Teach for America Corps member before embarking on her legal career, Temi is passionate about lifelong learning and combating socioeconomic disparities in minority communities.

When Temi is not helping people build successful businesses or exploring the latest legal tech and video tools, she is listening to music, trying out new restaurants, reading leadership books, and spending time with family and friends. To learn more about Temi Siyanbade and her work, visit www.temisiyanbade.com.

Index